MORE PRAISE FOR
TALES FROM A ROGUE RANGER

"Rosanne tells it like it is, with humor and wonderful details of the pains and joys of working as a California State Park Ranger. Fantastic park stories of people and Mother Nature are featured inside this fascinating peek at the world of a park ranger. Funny, intriguing, and a really good read!"

— **MIKE LYNCH**, retired California State Park Ranger and Historian.
Author of *Rangers of California State Parks: Over 125 Years of Protection and Service.*

"The presentation of real life experiences in this book glow with the revelations and frustrations of park rangers. Protecting the people from our parks and the parks from our people is a curious challenge unique to park rangers. Within the pages of this book is the madness and gladness of the profession."

— **CLIFF COLLIER**, National Park Service Protection Ranger.

TALES FROM *A ROGUE RANGER* IS THE SECOND
BOOK IN THE *TRIP TALES* SERIES.

McHenry's first book, *Trip Tales: From Family Camping to Life
as a Ranger,* is an award-winning read about how family camping
adventures as a child inspired her to become a National Park Ranger.

www.triptalesbook.com

TALES FROM A ROGUE RANGER

ROSANNE S. MCHENRY

Tales From a Rogue Ranger

Rosanne S. McHenry

Cover art by Joan Chlarson

ISBN (Print Edition): 979-8-35093-605-6

ISBN (eBook Edition): 979-8-35093-606-3

DEDICATION

For my husband,
'Ranger Vern',
and for our grandsons,
George and Remington.

CONTENTS

INTRODUCTION

I loved being a park ranger. My first book *Trip Tales: From Family Camping to Life as a Ranger*, details my early adventures as a National Park Ranger at Golden Gate National Recreation Area in Marin, California, and at Mount Rainier National Park in Washington State. What had begun as a volunteer job as a geology student from San Francisco State University led to a career with the National Park Service, and later, to a career with the California Department of Parks and Recreation. I eventually went back to work with the National Park Service many years later at Death Valley National Park in California, a spectacular place to be a park ranger in the winter months.

My park ranger duties in the National Park Service involved generalist work. I did guided-walks and talks, resource management, and visitor rescues. The work was fun and rewarding, low stress, and always enjoyable.

My work as a California State Park Ranger was very different. From "Nature Guide" to "Wilderness Cop" I became a full-time peace officer with all the "tools of the trade" worn around my belt, and a star-shaped law enforcement badge on my shirt. I was no longer giving guided walks; now I was patrolling large recreation parks and backcountry areas, enforcing laws, protecting the parks, and the people in them. The job could get very interesting at times. In fact, it was extremely challenging, and often daunting. I never knew what was going to happen next, and every day was literally an adventure.

Why the title: *Tales from a Rogue Ranger*? Surviving in this job meant you had to approach the job with an intrepid mindset. I took great pride and honor in the work I did, but I had to be bold to defend the wide open spaces under my care. These are stories of my wild years patrolling the American River Canyon in the Sierra Nevada Foothills.

PROLOGUE

The year was 1988 at the Auburn State Recreation Area in California's Sierra Nevada foothills. Two veteran rangers stood outside the office under the tall pine trees. They were good friends who had worked together for many years. Like most of the rangers I worked with at that park, they were strong in stature and toughened by the physical and emotional demands of the job. They reminisced in the afternoon light, thinking back across the years.

"I never realized how great the responsibility was, being a ranger" the first one said.

"When I initially took the job, I had no idea what I was getting myself into."

"How so, buddy?" his friend asked.

"I thought it would be easy, like a walk in the proverbial park," he smiled wanly. "But it was never like that. Instead, I had to put on police gear and go out into the parks to protect people … from each other."

"I know what you mean" his friend replied. "It was always a challenge, wasn't it?"

"Yeah. We had to be ready for anything, anytime. We didn't know if we would be doing something easy, like identifying a wildflower for a curious kid, or deadly dangerous, like drawing a gun to save someone from a shooter!"

"I know; it was like that most days," his friend said. "It was always an adventure. I lost count of how many times I set fractures, rescued drowning swimmers, broke up fights, counseled troubled kids, chased down drug dealers, investigated crimes, and recovered bodies. You just never knew what would happen next."

"Yeah; it was crazy for sure! Sometimes I wonder why I took the job, much less stayed on over the years. Why do any of us do this job? But you know, there were good days too, many good days. Times when we really helped people, times when it felt so great to be there for them. I'm pretty sure I'd do it all over again, given the chance. It was a calling."

They climbed into the patrol truck and drove down into the American River Canyon. Along the way they passed tall Ponderosa pine trees with their branches reaching up to the deep blue sky. Water cascaded downhill, tumbling into the river below. Yellow California poppies and blue lupine poked out between blades of green spring grass along the canyon walls. A railroad train sighed in the distance. It was early May at the Auburn State Recreation Area, a 40,000-acre park along the North and Middle Forks of the American River encompassing steep, forested canyons, and wild stretches of river.

When they reached an overlook across the Middle Fork they got out and looked across the canyon. A straight section of the river stretched for a mile south before it turned west again. They stood together in silence for a moment.

"You know the thing I remember most about the job?"

"What's that, buddy?"

"When I heard a park visitor tell me: "Thank God you're here!" Hearing things like this made all the hard aspects of the job worthwhile. Of all the things we rangers do, and of all the things I've ever had to do, that single sentence rings the loudest in my memory. They were so glad to see me that day, those park visitors, so glad to have a ranger arrive on scene. I can't even recall what the incident was about. I just remember their anxious faces and hearing them exclaim:

"Thank God you're here!"

1.
A RIOT OF A TIME!

It was a screamingly hot summer day at Folsom Lake State Recreation Area in the Sierra Nevada foothills of California. This twenty thousand-acre park situated in the rolling oak woodlands of the American River was a popular gathering spot for the greater Sacramento, California area. The North and South Forks of the American River meet at the 340-foot-tall Folsom Dam, creating a lake with seventy-five miles of shoreline. It was a popular place for picnicking, boating, swimming, camping, hiking, riding, and many other types of recreation. Because of its location, it drew families, friends ... and lots of partying teenagers. Much of the time it was a nice place to be, but on hot summer days, things could get pretty crazy.

The year was 1986, and I was a young park ranger. On a busy weekend it was common to see at least ten thousand people in the park. There were people everywhere, most of them drinking, fighting, swimming, boating, shouting, cursing, laughing, screaming, hollering, and generally raising hell. I never understood why young people enjoyed congregating in such huge groups. When I was a kid, I craved solitude. But I guess I must have been a strange kid. Then I grew up and became a California State Park Ranger, and it was my job to deal with all of the madness.

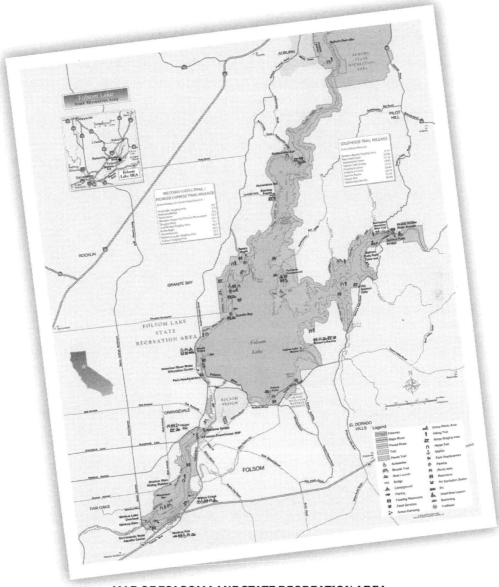

**MAP OF FOLSOM LAKE STATE RECREATION AREA,
COURTESY OF CALIFORNIA STATE PARKS –
PARKS.CA.GOV, PUBLIC DOMAIN**

Park visitors loved the party scene and would gather in huge numbers at Main Granite Beach. This was a central location in the park with
a big, crescent-shaped bay, a boat launch area, snack bar, restrooms, and a

picnic area surrounded by an oak forest. Loud music blasted, and beachgoers were packed tightly together on colorful blankets and towels. Beautiful young women in thong bikinis strolled the shore, attracting the attention of everyone in the area.

Back then, people were allowed to bring alcohol to the beach. Eventually, alcohol was banned to reduce crime in the park. But in the 1980s, it was still a wild scene. As alcohol consumption skyrocketed, simple reason turned to uncontrolled rage.

"Whaddya think you're doing staring at us like that?" one guy shouted.

"I wasn't looking at you, jerk! I was checking out the water behind you!" said another guy.

"You were checking out my girlfriend. You wanna check out my fist?"

"Oh yeah? Come over here and I'll knock the crap out of you!"

Before long, the formerly idyllic scene, with lake waves lapping quietly against the shore and happy picnickers relaxing on beach blankets, turned into a violent riot with people shouting, knives flashing, and fists smashing. It was amazing how quickly this happened, like a tidal wave cresting from one end of the beach to the other, carrying everyone along and churning into a massive altercation.

Big knots of people were suddenly engulfed in mass fights. Why people acted this way was beyond my understanding. I *loathed* the hot summer days here because the high temperatures brought the biggest and wildest crowds to the park. The popular police TV shows had nothing on us Folsom Lake rangers. We saw every kind of crime imaginable every day.

Most people think of Smokey the Bear when they imagine a park ranger, but California State Park Rangers are fully qualified peace officers like any other. We experienced fights, drownings, serious boat injuries, bloody car accidents, screaming parents with missing children, shootings, domestic violence, aggravated assault, death threats, and every other type of incident.

Often, the rangers had to step in and break up fights before people literally killed each other. One of our rangers was a dog handler with a fearsome-looking German shepherd named Max. When he appeared on the scene, most miscreants stopped being jerks and quickly decided to behave. But the dog handler wasn't always available to help. Sometimes he was busy elsewhere in the park, and we had to handle things alone.

On days like this, when I was alone, I'd get so fed up with this asinine, juvenile behavior that I'd lose my cool. I remember one incident when a group of about forty young men in shorts and T-shirts were throwing punches at each other. I threw all caution aside and angrily stormed straight into the center of this huge fight, screaming at everyone.

"Knock this off *right now* or you are all going to jail!" Heads whirled around at the craziness of the insane woman ranger wading right into the midst of a forty-person battle.

"If you think I'm kidding, just try me! Who wants to go to jail right now?"

"Jeez, that woman is nuts! What's her deal?" several of the young men said in wonderment.

"I dunno, but we'd better get the hell outta here right now!"

People took off in every direction as the fight rapidly dissipated.

"Who wants a free trip to jail?" I shouted at those who were left. "Who started this mess, anyway?"

Looks of incredulity passed between the remaining players as the crowd dispersed.

"Uh, he did. That little guy right over there."

"That tiny little dude? He started all this?"

"Yep."

"Why?"

"Dunno."

The perpetrator lay there in the sand, bleeding from countless punches. He was slim and small with sandy-colored hair, clad in a torn black T-shirt and blue jean shorts. He was pretty clueless because he was still mouthing insults at the remaining people standing around.

"Come back and fight, you dipshits!"

"Shut up, stupid! Don't you know when to stop?" one of his friends said.

With the help of his buddies, I wearily pulled the kid to his feet and walked him back to my car to treat his injuries. He wasn't hurt badly, just bruised. I checked him for injuries and cleaned up his cuts with alcohol wipes and bandages.

"What did you say to make people so mad at you?" I asked him.

"They were disrespecting me! I won't let no one disrespect me!"

"You're a fool, little dude," I told him. "Be quiet right now or I will haul you off to jail for starting this fight."

When ego-driven young men get into a fight, they don't think about the impact their aggression can have on others. Sometimes a single punch can have devastating consequences for everyone involved. When we as park rangers step in to stop a fight, it's often to save lives. I didn't like having to take a tough stance like this, but sometimes it was the only thing young men understood.

I glared at the little group of four friends. "Look, guys, the fight's over. I can take you all to jail for inciting a riot, or you can just take this kid and go home. Which is it?"

"We'll be on our way right now, ma'am."

"Good idea," I replied.

I wondered why young men acted this way, but I realized it was just basic primate instinct. Alcohol, drugs, too many people crowded into one area—it was the perfect storm for fights. Humans are still pretty much like chimpanzees. Actually, I think the chimps may be smarter, especially when it comes to raging hormones and teenage posturing. This always seemed to happen when it was one hundred degrees or more outside. *Why can't everyone just jump into the lake and cool off?* I wondered. *And why on earth had I decided to become a patrol ranger?*

When I first began my career as a ranger, I envisioned being out in nature leading happy guided walks and talks with park visitors, talking about our rich natural and cultural heritage. My early years were like that, working in places like the Golden Gate National Recreation Area in California and Mount Rainier National Park in Washington State. I understood that law enforcement would be part of the job someday if I chose a patrol ranger position, but I never envisioned this level of mayhem.

The next afternoon, the park dispatchers told me that all through the high school grapevine I was known as the Crazy Woman Ranger. One dispatcher, Mary, had a son in the local high school, so she was always privy to the latest teenage news.

"My son told me you broke up a big fight at Main Granite Beach yesterday," she said. "He was watching from the sidelines as you stormed into the midst of the battle. He said that you're insane, and all the kids are afraid of you."

"Good!" I told her.

I didn't like shouting at people, but sometimes this was the only way to stop a dangerous fight. The "friendly ranger" approach didn't work too well when you were trying to quell a riot.

"How did you get them to stop fighting?" Mary asked.

"Why don't you come with me on a ride-along and see firsthand what I do?" I offered.

"Okay," Mary said, clearly intrigued. "I've always wanted to see things actually happening out there."

The next day I gave her the full-spectrum tour of the beach, the campground, the picnic areas, and the remote backcountry areas. Along the way I dealt with two big fights, three illegal firearms contacts, four citations, and a vehicle stop for drunk driving. Mary watched in wide-eyed horror.

When I waded into a group of five men at Cherokee Bar to take away rifles for shooting at hawks, this was too much for her. Finally, she cried:

"Please take me back to Dispatch now. I've seen enough. I don't know how you rangers can stand to do this job! You certainly have all my sympathies and support. Now, please, let's go back; I can't bear to watch anymore. How you manage to stay alive out here is beyond comprehension."

I respected Mary's request and took her straight back to headquarters. The dispatchers were an outstanding group who often saved our lives when they heard tension building on the radio. More than once they dispatched additional officers to the scene without being asked when they sensed we were getting in over our heads.

Dealing with bad behavior at parties was a regular part of being a ranger, even at night.

2.
NIGHT PARTY

One night my partner Daryl and I were on a late patrol on Auburn Folsom Road when we came across a big party at Beal's Point, just upstream from the main Folsom Dam. The parties happened frequently. You might wonder: what's the harm of kids partying by a lake at night? Why did we have to break up their fun? All kids need a place to blow off steam sometimes, right? But we couldn't just ignore it. To do so would be negligence, because the kids drank heavily, then they drove around drunk, posing a serious threat of injury to themselves and others. The safest option was to try and stop them in the act.

Our strategy was to sneak up on the kids before they could scatter and get away. First, we wrote absentee parking tickets for all the cars illegally parked on the roadway below the saddle dam at Beal's Point. There was a wide section of beach on the other side, hidden from view. The kids figured if they didn't drive into the park entrance and just scrambled up over the saddle dam, no one would notice they were there. But the string of cars parked all along the base of the dam was like a screaming beacon: "Come party here!"

Once we finished leaving our "calling cards" on the cars, we made our way up the back of the dam so we could pounce on the unsuspecting kids gathered along the beach at the lakeside below. They had a crackling bonfire and a keg of beer. Music played merrily from their boom box and we could hear about thirty of them talking and laughing. But the crafty little devils had posted a lookout. When they heard us coming, the lookout shouted a warning, and everyone bolted. Many slipped away in the darkness, leaving their booze behind on the beach.

I was so hopping mad at this unfortunate turn of events! How *dare* they run from us? I was already exhausted from a very long, hot day and was in no mood to go chasing after errant juveniles. It was dark, and they were young and fast, like gazelles. Still, we managed to trap about a dozen of the kids as they came running in our direction.

"Dammit, they're gonna run right past us!" Daryl exclaimed.

"No, they won't!" I shouted.

"What are you gonna do?"

"Just watch me and go along with it, okay?"

"Oh jeez, Rosanne! Why does this worry me?"

"Just follow my lead."

As the kids ran toward us, I hollered out: "Stop in your tracks right now or you're all going straight to jail!" I shouted as loud as I could. "We have you surrounded!"

It was just Daryl and me, but the kids didn't know this. They all stopped dead in their tracks. All they could see were the beams from our flashlights boring deep into their shocked eyeballs. We each held up two flashlights to confuse them into thinking there were at least four of us.

"If even one of you tries to run you are going to be seriously sorry!" I screamed at them. "Form a line! Do it *now!*"

The kids hastily lined up like kindergartners on the playground.

"March forward, slowly! We are going back down the hill to the patrol cars. Do exactly as I say! You got that? Say yes, ma'am!"

"Yes, ma'am," they all replied shakily as we marched down the hill.

When we got back to the road, Daryl and I drove the kids the quarter mile back to the park entrance station and lined them up outside.

"We are calling your parents to come pick you up. I want each of you to give us your home phone numbers when we ask, or you are going straight to jail!"

It was 11:00 at night. Twelve home phone numbers were immediately called. The angry but grateful parents came to pick up their errant children, threatening them with being grounded for the rest of their lives. All of the parents thanked us.

Afterward, Daryl looked at me and said, "You know, Rosanne, you scared the hell out of me, too."

"Good!" I laughed out loud. "Fear is good." Then we both laughed uncontrollably at the absurdity of the whole event.

The next day, the dispatcher said, "What is it with you? Every kid in the district is terrified of this crazy woman ranger!"

"Good," I said again and smiled. Maybe we had saved some lives.

3.

LET COOLER
HEADS PREVAIL

On really busy weekends we tried to stop party trouble at its source. Underage drinkers rolled into the Main Granite Beach parking lot with coolers full of alcohol. We strolled over to them as they unloaded the coolers.

"Mind if we take a look at what's inside?" we'd ask.

"Uh, okay," most of them would say. A lot of them didn't know they had the right to refuse, but if they did start screaming about their rights, we would tell them they'd be followed out to the beach, and then it would be ticket time for anyone under the age of twenty-one in possession of alcohol. We'd open up their coolers, revealing treasure chests stuffed with bottled beer, wine coolers, hard liquor, and other alcoholic beverages.

"Let's see some ID for the alcohol," we'd say.

"We didn't bring any," was the common answer.

"Well then, if you have no way to prove you are over twenty-one, I guess you're going to have to leave the alcohol here."

"What?" the kids would holler. "You can't just take our stuff! You just want it for yourselves!" they would cry out.

"We don't want your booze. Instead, we are going to let you pour it out yourselves, right here and now."

"The cooler belongs to our uncle, and he's twenty-five! He'll be here any minute."

"Your uncle is contributing to the delinquency of minors and will be arrested if he comes over here to claim this cooler."

"You jerk rangers!"

"Would you prefer to go to jail? You have three choices: pour the alcohol out right now, get a ticket, or win a free trip to jail."

"Can't we just turn around and leave now?"

"Sure, but first you have to pour out the alcohol."

"Jeez! You rangers really suck!" they'd shout as they poured out their booze onto the hot, sizzling, unforgiving pavement. "What are we supposed to drink? It's really hot out here!"

"The snack bar is right over there. They sell sodas and water. Enjoy your stay."

We gathered more bounty as we patrolled the beach. Almost every beach blanket was accompanied by a brightly-colored cooler.

"We need to see some ID for this cooler full of alcohol," we'd say.

"It belongs to our buddy, and he is thirty-two, but he just walked down the beach. Not sure where he is at the moment." They snickered at their own cleverness.

"You mean your buddy left minors in charge of the alcohol? We'll just take the cooler as evidence."

"You can't take that; it's not yours!"

"Are you twenty-one? Apparently, it's not yours either, right? So, you won't object if we take your buddy's stuff to keep him and you from getting in trouble, right?"

Speechless glares.

By the end of each week, we had so many empty coolers in our ready room there was hardly any place left to walk. It was a veritable maze of coolers stacked five feet high. We took them to the local thrift shops and Goodwill stores, but after a while, they had no more room for them, either. There was no reason to keep these as evidence; no judge ever asked to see coolers. What to do with them all? Finally, we contacted the local Elks clubs and other philanthropic organizations so they could use them for summer picnic fundraisers. The clubs loved them.

This was recycling at its best! Still, we wondered what we could do to try to cut down on the underage drinking at the park.

4.

UNDERCOVER BLUES

There was so much trouble with kids partying at Folsom Lake and upstream on the American River that we decided to try an undercover operation to flush them out of the area once and for all. I contacted our law enforcement deputy director.

"Will, what do you think about staging an undercover operation to shake these kids up?"

"I don't know, Rosanne. These things don't always work. They can backfire and then you are in worse shape than before."

"We need to do something about it, Will. These kids are carrying on every weekend and the problem keeps getting worse. They hide their alcohol and drugs in the rocks and river, which makes it difficult to conduct a search. We can bluff our way through a search and pour out their booze, but the local courts won't support our efforts. They throw out all our charges, and the kids keep coming back. We need to do something to expose these offenders and scare them off. They are a hazard to themselves and everyone they see. They could crack their skulls on the slippery rocks. We can't sneak up on them because there is no cover. They can see us coming from a half mile away. If you go in undercover and act like you want to party with them, maybe you can gather enough evidence to flush them out for good."

"He let out a long sigh. Well, we can try. I'll get a couple of guys together, and we'll see what we can do."

"Thanks, Will," I said hopefully. My ranger staff were keen on this idea and couldn't wait to see it happen.

Later that month Will came up with two other guys from the law enforcement unit. They were dressed in swim trunks, T-shirts, and ball caps and brought a cooler with them as a prop. They spotted plenty of unlawful activity before they went in, just by standing on the bridge above the river pool where the youngsters gathered. The kids were partying and carrying on, and as they drank more, they became belligerent and began to threaten other park visitors walking by. Will and the guys ambled down onto the rocks to join the miscreant gang, but it didn't take long until the kids smelled a rat. These guys were obviously not from around the area, and the local kids knew it. After about ten minutes the game was up.

"Rosanne, you may as well come down here," Will said into the radio. "It didn't take them long to figure out we don't belong."

"On my way, Will. Did you at least scare them a bit?"

"Not really. They invited us to stay and party."

I hiked down and talked with the group. Will and his buddies had become pals with the kid-brats, and they were all standing around talking and laughing.

"Don't worry about it, Rosanne," Will told me. "I have a feeling you may have accomplished your objective. Let's see what happens."

I just wish those kids would grow up, I thought to myself. *Why can't they just act responsibly?* Then I thought back to when I was a kid and some of the stupid things I did. They were just being youngsters, I figured. Someday they would grow up. At least I hoped so.

In the end, the gambit worked. The local kids decided it wasn't worth it to party at the river with all the ranger oversight. We simply caused them too much trouble. From then on, they stayed outside of the park to party. But there was no guarantee we wouldn't have the same problem somewhere else.

5.

THE DRUG USER

One day my coworkers at the Auburn ranger station asked me to help them out with an undercover sting operation.

"We need someone to dress up as a drug user and watch what's going on at the confluence," my supervisor told me.

Being the only woman ranger on staff, I was the one chosen for this singular honor. They needed a fellow ranger who could play the role convincingly enough but not be spotted as a law enforcement officer.

The confluence is where the North and Middle Forks of the American River meet, and where the Highway 49 Bridge crosses the river near Auburn. The river forms lovely, emerald green pools and cascading rapids against the backdrop of steep canyon walls. It was a popular spot all year long and especially in the summer, where triple-digit temperatures drew people of all ages to the shore. Teenage drinkers and drug users also frequented the area, and we kept a close eye on this activity.

"We want you to dress up as a drinker and drug user!" Jordan (one of the other rangers) laughed. "That way you'll fit right in with the local drinkers and dopers, and you can see up close what's going on. We keep trying to observe the kids down there, but they always spot us. If you go there and spot them, we can easily go in and pop them for drinking and drugs."

"A drinker and drug user? Don't you think you're getting a little carried away with this ideology?" I asked him.

"We like the idea," he laughed.

I wasn't too keen on this idea, but I also didn't want to be a naysayer. The guys often helped me when I needed an extra hand, and it wouldn't be right for me to say no at this point.

"Okay, guys, I'll help you out, but don't leave me out in the hot sun too long or forget about me while you go off and do something else." I knew too well how quickly they could get distracted by something more exciting.

They dropped me off on the roadway above the bridge, and I walked down to the river where some kids were partying. I did my best to look as slimy and lawless as I possibly could in my ripped T-shirt and ragged-looking shorts. I staggered toward the river's edge acting drunk, and sat there in the hot sun with a whiskey bottle in my hand, watching dozens of teenage kids drinking, partying, and generally acting foolishly. My coworkers took forever getting to the scene. Finally, I walked off to the bushes where I couldn't be seen and radioed them.

"Where the heck are you?" I demanded. "I've been sitting down here for almost an hour!"

"Sorry, we got involved in a vehicle stop. We're here now. What have you witnessed?"

"A bunch of teens drinking and smoking weed. Way too many of them are falling down drunk, and I worry that some of them are going to drop into the river and drown later. Let's get this done so I can get out of the sun. It must be 115 degrees down here!"

"Quiet, you're just a druggie!" (Laughter in the radio background).

Hmmm, I thought. They were getting just a little *too* into character with all this. I decided this was the *last* time I would work undercover. It sucked.

"Okay, Rosanne, which kid is it? This one? This one? How about this one?"

They held up their ball caps over the kids in question, so I could see them from a distance. Once I identified the underage drinkers, Ike and Jordan wrote the citations, which I later signed. This went on for the better part of *another hour* as I finally quit the act and walked over to assist them.

Back at the office, Jordan couldn't help himself.

"What's it like being a druggie? You sure look like one in that garb!"

"Yeah, you look pretty damn badass in those cutoffs. We might have to haul you to jail!" one of the others said.

The ranger office at Auburn had the reputation of being "The Home of the Cold Shot." You had to be tough to work there and weather the shots, but this was getting to be a bit too much, even for a war-hardened field veteran like me.

"Guys, it's time to break character. This 'doper' is officially off duty as of right now. Now knock it off, and don't invite me on an undercover operation again. I have enough to contend with at this job as it is. Game over and out." Then I dragged my poor, overheated body into my car and drove home in my ripped-up shirt and ragged shorts. On the way back I received curious stares from other drivers looking through the window at my crazy hair and torn shirt. When I got out of the car in front of my house, my neighbors took one look at me and laughed out loud.

"Did you just come from work? You look like a drug user! What's up with that outfit? Should we call the police?"

"Go ahead," I replied tiredly. "At least then someone else can do the paperwork."

How do I let myself get talked into these things? I wondered. This was the last time I would ever do something like this. But I had to admit, it *was* funny!

6.
DON'T JUMP!

Party groups at the river were one thing, but bridge jumpers were a constant aggravation to park rangers. Local bridges spanned the river along the three forks of the American River near the towns of Colfax, Auburn, and Placerville. Teenaged kids, stoked on alcohol and drugs, often believed they were invincible. They did crazy things like jump off bridges twenty or thirty feet high, landing in water that was often too shallow, too fast, or filled with unseen obstacles. Drownings happened every year.

A popular party spot was the Ponderosa Bridge on the North Fork of the American River near Colfax. A long, winding road led down to a pony truss bridge where a deep, green pool and a pleasant sandy beach awaited. Tall canyon walls rose up on either side. The Ponderosa Bridge stood thirty-five feet above the river, and the water ran about fifteen feet deep under the 222-foot-long span. (This was replaced in late 2023 by a more modern bridge.)

I used to dread driving up to this spot because every summer weekend it was the same: at least one hundred people in the area with twenty-five to thirty young men hanging off the bridge performing ridiculous antics to impress the bikini-clad girls on the beach below. The guys would swing from the support beams like chimpanzees, hooting and hollering, then jump outward, bellowing primal screams as they sailed through the air into the river below. When they came up for air, their drunken compatriots howled with delight, urging their favorite primates to jump again and again.

Humanity hasn't come far in the last two hundred thousand years, I mused as I surveyed the scene. We are still just as dumb as ever. In fact, I think the apes are way ahead of us at this point.

OLD PONDEROSA WAY BRIDGE NEAR COLFAX, CALIFORNIA

Bridge jumping was illegal. There were signs everywhere proclaiming this. The idea was to keep kids from smacking their heads open on the limestone rocks below. We were continually called to the scene to rescue injured jumpers. Broken legs and drownings happened every summer. But the youngsters could not resist the desire to be daredevils. Every youth believed he would live forever. Emphasis on *"he."* Rarely did I see a young woman do this. They didn't need to impress anyone by jumping.

Whenever I went to the bridge, I always arranged to have another ranger meet me on the opposite side so that we could block the exodus of traffic in both directions while we advanced on the group. This allowed us to trap the kids, so we could pick off the ringleaders and make public examples of them. Once we were positioned in place, we would hit the area with a loudspeaker as the sound waves bounced off the rocky canyon walls all around.

"Everyone get down off the bridge! Do it *now!*" we would shout through the loudspeaker.

Curious looks and stares filled the silence that followed.

"Get down off the bridge immediately, or you will be arrested!"

Then the kids slowly clambered off the bridge, making rude hand gestures and mouthing colorful metaphors.

"Get into your cars and leave the area immediately or you will be cited or arrested. Clear the area. Do it now!"

"F—k you!" one of the dumber ones would shout, believing that the clueless rangers would have no idea who uttered this epithet. But we'd spotted the ringleaders in advance. We already knew who the challengers were, who were the loudest, the most profane, the most obnoxious, the most problematic, and we were ready for them. We'd march right into the center of the group and pull the troublemakers from the huddle, hand-cuffing them and stuffing them into the back of our patrol cars. Then we would line up the rest of the kids and do an identity check on each one. Some of the more deserving ones received citations.

The seductive girls in bikinis tried to sweet-talk my partners into not writing tickets, but I'd collar them with great glee saying, "That stuff doesn't work too well with me, girl. Just let them do their job, or you will go to jail for interfering with the lawful duties of a peace officer."

Then we rapidly distributed citations.

One by one we let the kids loose, releasing them to their cars to depart the area. The ringleaders were transported to juvenile hall. Word would get out and things would be quiet for a while, but the problem always came back. Some days we'd drive up to a bridge and hear shouts of alarm.

"Jimmy broke his leg!"

"Stuart busted his skull open. He's not answering us!"

"Billy did this awesome triple flip, but then he hit that tree stump near the bridge post. I think he has a busted back!"

And so on. The reckless stupidity of it all never ceased to amaze me.

Most people don't understand the powerful force of moving water and how it can pin you down or carry you under. I completed an El Dorado County Sheriff's swift water rescue course that spring. We had to dive into moving water, "rescue" our buddies and pull them from the waves, pull ourselves out from under hidden debris (strainers), and recover from slipping and "falling" into rapids. I was in top physical shape at the time and imagined it would be very easy to work through these exercises. *Wrong!*

Swiftly moving water is unpredictable. Just the sheer force of five thousand cubic feet per second, or even half that amount, can sweep a person underwater in a millisecond and pin them down until they drown. I was absolutely shocked that I couldn't pull myself over a simple submerged rope, much less fight my way out of a multipronged strainer. It was a real eye-opening experience for me.

We also had to go down the river in a raft, then swim to safety when our instructors purposely flipped the boat over. I wore a helmet and life jacket and remembered thinking it would be so easy to swim to safety once I was dumped into the river. Instead, I got pinned against a rock and had to wait for one of the other "rescuers" to throw me a rope and pull me to safety. Talk about a paradigm shift! Yikes. Moving water is a powerful force.

Sometimes I'd sit on the shore and shout to people in rafts going by, "Put your lifejackets on!"

It amazed me how countless people would climb into a plastic raft and careen downriver with nothing to keep them afloat if they ended up in the water. Half of them couldn't even swim! It was ridiculous, yet we saw this every day. In fact, I'd been guilty of the same clueless behavior years before I became a ranger, when I went on a river trip with friends. We hadn't even worn life jackets because we thought we could swim to safety if we fell out of the boat. We had no idea of the dangers then.

The worst water-related death trap was at the confluence of the North and Middle Forks just below Auburn. Sandy beaches beckoned sun worshippers to the picturesque spot, and a whole patchwork of humanity congregated near this Highway 49 bridge crossing. People came to picnic, swim, and wade into the river. Most folks had fun for the day and departed unscathed. But every season there were casualties, especially when water was released from the Oxbow Dam miles upstream, causing a rapid and unexpected rise in river level. This caught people off guard. One minute people were laughing and standing in a couple feet of water, and the next minute they were swept downstream. It made no difference if the person was a strong swimmer. It also didn't matter how old they were. Strong young men were swept off their feet. Often, they'd regain their balance, but then get caught in floating debris and be pulled underwater again. It happened so fast—in milliseconds. Friends and family members trying to save each other were often swept away as well. We'd hear comments like these all the time:

"Robbie was right there! Just a moment ago! Now he's gone! *Gone!* We didn't even see it happen!"

"Phil was standing right there! Then water seemed to come out of nowhere. It dragged all our stuff into the river. Tom stepped into the river to help Phil, and then they both got pulled away from shore. Tom swam after Phil, but he couldn't catch up to him. Then they both went underwater. It happened so fast! Where'd they go?"

Nature is indifferent. Rushing water and centrifugal force can claim lives in an instant.

7.

JUST HANGIN' AROUND

My husband, Vern, was also a park ranger. We worked on many of the same assignments over the years. We often traded stories or commiserated after particularly harrowing incidents. It was a good way to decompress after a difficult week and to learn from each other's experiences.

One Christmas Day Vern got a call from Dispatch that someone tragically hung themselves from the Auburn-Foresthill Bridge. Standing 730 feet above the American River Canyon floor, this bridge is as high above the American River as the Golden Gate Bridge is above the San Francisco Bay. When it was first constructed, there were plans to build the Auburn Dam about a mile downstream, which would have created a deep lake beneath the bridge. But opposition to building the dam was so great that it was never constructed. So, the bridge stands high above the canyon floor. Every year desperate people committed suicide by leaping to their deaths. It was horrifying. As of July 2023, there have been over one hundred deaths. Recent retrofits to the bridge included a much higher fence and call boxes to deter suicides.

But on that Christmas Day, it was the first time someone had hung themselves from the bridge. It just didn't make any sense.

"How can it be?" I asked. "How could someone manage to do this? Wouldn't they have to climb way down onto the catwalk? Isn't it impossible to do that? The staff keeps the access door to the catwalk locked, right?"

"I don't know how they did this. I'll have to go see," he replied morosely.

"I'm so sorry!" I said. "What a heartbreaking thing to have to deal with, especially on Christmas Day! Do you want me to come with you?"

"No, please stay home; it can't be helped," he said as he got ready to leave.

I was so upset. That poor person! What a tragedy for their family! It was Christmas, and news about a death would be extremely difficult to hear, and a suicide even harder. It was almost too much to bear even thinking about it. And my poor husband had to go deal with it.

An hour later my husband returned home. To my amazement, he was chuckling to himself.

"How can you be laughing about a suicide?" I asked with incredulity. His eyes were filled with mirth.

"Because it wasn't a suicide," he replied, somewhat mystically.

"What do you mean?"

"It was a dummy!"

"That's no way to talk about the dead!"

"No, really, it was a dummy! A mannequin."

"What? How?"

He couldn't stop laughing long enough to tell me. By then, our twelve-year-old daughter had come into the room to listen.

"Dad, did someone kill themselves?"

"No, Honey. Someone hung a dummy from the bridge!"

"How?" we both cried.

"They must have taken it from the decoy California Highway Patrol [CHP] car parked near the train trestle on Highway 80."

The CHP kept a decoy patrol car with a dummy in it near the train trestle over Highway 80 at the west end of Auburn. The decoy was supposed to slow down traffic passing through town. Apparently, some enterprising youngsters broke into the car and abducted "Officer Dummy." Then they took it up to the Foresthill Bridge.

The catwalk is accessed through a doorway on the west side of the bridge, which was kept locked. But, near the middle of the bridge there were cables suspended along the length of the structure. Able-bodied people could climb down, lower themselves from the cable, and get onto the catwalk. However, this stunt was exceedingly dangerous. One slip and the climber could fall to their death over seven hundred feet below.

The kids who tied the dummy to the catwalk with a noose around its neck were true aerial artists in the most macabre way. They managed to clamber way out onto the edge of the catwalk with the dummy, which was very heavy. Then, they tied the rope around its neck and looped this over the support beam without dropping the dummy in the process. It was sheer, diabolical genius.

My husband told me:

"At first, we were really upset because we saw the body hanging twenty feet beneath the bridge catwalk. It was swaying in the breeze and looked so life-like. The wind was blowing its hair, and it had a realistic-looking face on it. We saw the CHP uniform and were even more upset to think that a fellow officer had committed suicide.

AUBURN FORESTHILL BRIDGE IN BACKGROUND, TAKEN FROM OLD FORESTHILL ROAD

"We were trying to decide what to do: haul the body up, or cut it down and let it fall to the river below, then retrieve it afterward. We would have cut it down, but there were too many spectators on the bridge and they would have been horrified if it had fallen into the river. It was very tricky and dangerous because we had to step out onto the catwalk and risk our lives retrieving it. The CHP helicopter and television news copters were circling around, trying to get a closer look at their fallen comrade. But the prop wash (wind current created by the whirring helicopter blades) kept spinning the body around so no one could get a close look at it.

"We climbed down and worked hard to haul the body up. It was so heavy! We were hoping it wasn't a CHP officer we knew. We didn't realize it was a dummy until we pulled it up and noticed that the hands were fake. Then we saw that it still had all the sales tags attached to the uniform!

"We managed to cut the thing loose, drag it off the catwalk, and haul it up onto the bridge. It weighed a ton, it was hard to keep from falling, and there was a huge crowd on the bridge watching the incident, including news reporters with television cameras. Those kids who did this upset a lot of people."

"What did you do with the dummy?" I couldn't help but ask.

"We turned it over to the CHP. It was their dummy, after all."

"I'm sorry, babe, that you had to go through all that, especially on Christmas Day."

"I'm just glad it wasn't a real body!" he sighed in relief.

Officer Dummy never returned to duty in the patrol car, although the car remained in place beneath the bridge for a couple more years.

8.
WILD GOOSE CHASE

Not all crimes in parks have to do with people. Sometimes the perpetrator is a creature. I remember this story so clearly because it happened to my husband, Vern, and I was the one who gave him first aid when he came home with his legs all bloodied.

One afternoon Vern was called to the scene of a killer goose. Between Folsom Dam and the smaller Nimbus Dam below, there is a ten-mile stretch of water known as Lake Natoma. At the upper end of the lake is the campground and day-use area called Miner's Bar.

On this fateful afternoon, a group of terrified picnickers were being held hostage on top of a picnic table. Their terrorist was an attack goose. The giant bird was patrolling around and around the table, daring anyone to step down. Anytime someone tried to set a foot on the ground to escape, the goose would attack them and sink its sharp beak into their legs hard enough to draw blood.

When Vern got the call from Dispatch, he laughed out loud.

"Ranger 616: Respond immediately to a report of six people trapped on top of a picnic table at Miner's Bar."

"Why are they trapped on top of a table?" he asked. "Did the lake flood?"

"Apparently, there is a wild goose attacking the group."

"A goose? Are you sure?"

Typically, geese ran *away* from people, not at them. Generally, geese did not perpetrate guerrilla warfare on park visitors.

"Affirmative, 616. You have an attack goose. Please respond immediately and subdue the bird."

"En route," he replied, laughing the whole way there. But when he arrived, he saw that the story was no hoax. As he walked down to the lakeside picnic area, he saw a large goose patrolling around a picnic table. On top of the table was a group of frightened people. The goose violently attacked anyone trying to leave.

"Help us, Ranger!" the captives shouted. "But be careful; this goose is crazy!"

"I'll soon sort this out," Vern stated confidently, as he swaggered up to the table. He'd show this goose who was in charge! At this precise moment, the goose went in for the kill. It darted out and sank its ragged beak into the ranger's right leg, drawing blood.

"Ouch!" he screamed out loud, looking at his bleeding leg in disbelief. He waved and shouted at the goose, but it kept flying at him and attacking. Soon, he joined the desultory group on top of the table. The wild bird resumed its patrol around the table, threatening anyone with great bodily harm if they dared to step down.

"How long have you all been standing here?" he asked the group.

"For almost an hour!" a man told him. "One man broke away and made a run for his car. The goose chased him all the way and really bloodied him up. It bit his legs, crashed against the guy's windshield, and dented his car doors with its beak, threatening to break in. That guy must be the one who called your dispatcher for help. He was so courageous!"

"I really need to go to the bathroom," a little girl wailed.

Good grief, thought Vern. He decided that the situation had escalated and that a show of superior force was now in order. He swung his baton at the goose, trying to scare it off. But this had no effect. It kept flying up and flapping its wings into his face. He tried grabbing the goose by the neck (which, according to wildlife experts, is the recommended method, but try telling that to the goose.) The giant bird just kept ducking and biting.

"Told you! Tried to warn you! It's a vicious animal!" the same man shouted.

"It's probably a parent with a nest nearby, which is why it's attacking us," Vern told the distraught man.

Clearly, this bird was not to be deterred. Vern radioed for animal control or wildlife rescue to come assist, but they were unavailable. He would have to deal with this situation on his own. He fervently wished for a giant bird net, but there was no way to get ahold of one, and he needed to rescue these people from captivity. Time to take it up a notch. He took out his pepper spray. The people on the table gasped in horror.

"Everyone, cover your eyes!" he shouted as he heroically leaped from the table, confronted his attacker and pepper sprayed the goose's head.

This stopped the goose cold. It spat, then gagged, then ran to the lakeside and ducked its head in the water, trying to wash the pepper spray off. Now this should have gotten rid of the goose, but no luck. After bobbing its head up and down in the water several times, it managed to rinse the pepper spray off, revive itself, and resume the attack.

"Yikes! It's coming back! Run to your cars! Do it *now!*" Vern shouted.

Everyone, including Vern, made a mad dash for their cars as the goose came charging after them. There was screaming and stumbling as the terrified park visitors ran for their lives. They barely managed to escape without further bloodshed.

The picnic area was closed off to visitors for the rest of the weekend. Finally, the goose was netted, its nest was located, and the entire goose family was relocated to a more remote area far away from people. Once the baby goslings were raised the goose would behave just like any other bird. Supposedly.

The terrifying reign of the killer goose had ended.

9.

THE FORGOTTEN PIG

Battling a wild goose was enough excitement for one season. The next week, an even crazier thing happened: someone dropped off a potbellied pig in the same picnic area. Ranger Vern couldn't believe it when the call came in over the radio.

"Ranger 616: respond to a report of an abandoned pig at Miner's Bar!"

"Abandoned pig? Dispatch, are you sure it's not a dog?"

"Negative, 616. It's a pig."

Good grief, he thought. *Why was he the one to always get these crazy calls? How did he get assigned to these ridiculous situations? It just didn't make any sense.* He headed over to Miner's Bar ... again. It was dusk when he arrived on the scene. A potbellied pig was wandering around the picnic area, snuffling, moaning, and looking very lost and confused.

Why would someone do this? he wondered. *Did it escape from a nearby yard?* This was unlikely, because there were many tract homes in the area. There were some mini farms nearby, though, and the chances were that some family moved away from the area and decided to "gift" the pig to the local state park. Unfortunately, dumping pets in the park was all too common. It was contemptible to abandon a poor animal like that, leaving it to fend for itself. Domesticated animals don't know how to forage for themselves. Dogs will often group together in packs and run wild. Cats can go feral and can easily find food. But a domesticated farm animal is generally quite helpless, and this poor pig was terrified.

An animal control officer soon joined Vern at the scene.

"What shall we do here? How are we going to capture this thing?" Vern asked the officer.

"Well, if we can get it into your truck, we can take it to a holding facility," the officer replied. "Let's see if we can grab it and lift it into the bed of your truck."

The two men tried herding the frightened pig toward the truck, but this immediately backfired. The traumatized animal started running in circles, squealing in terror. After ten minutes of trying in vain to capture it, the two men decided to regroup.

"Maybe what we need is a ramp to get it into the truck," Vern surmised. "I can go back to the maintenance shop and get some plank boards. It's just a few minutes up the road. Then we can set up a ramp into the truck."

"I have some animal feed in my vehicle. That will help us lure the pig up the ramp and into the truck. I always keep some critter food handy. Makes it a lot easier to get them to comply if you have something enticing to offer."

"Good idea," Vern said.

Fifteen minutes later they were ready to try out their plan.

"Be careful when we run the pig up the ramp so it doesn't trip and fall off the side!" the animal control officer warned.

But the pig had other ideas. Pigs are extremely clever and this one was no slouch. It looked at the ramp suspiciously and then ran away from them. They chased it around and around the area a few more times until Vern came up with a better idea. He grabbed a broom from the back of his truck and used this to gently herd the pig toward the ramp.

"I think this might work! Just help me chase it up the ramp!"

They put some animal feed into the truck bed, then gently coaxed and guided the pig up the ramp, but it stopped halfway up, looking confused about what to do next. It realized that if it continued into the truck bed it would be trapped, and this meant an uncertain future. The pig carefully considered this option and began to back down again.

"I'll hop into the truck bed with some feed in my hands, and maybe it will follow me in," Vern said. "I think it's just frightened and needs a friend."

"Dude, be careful! You don't know what the pig might do! They bite, you know!"

"It's nearly dark and we can't chase it all night," Vern said. "And we can't leave it here until morning because it could run onto the highway and cause an accident. We're running out of options."

"Okay, let's take it slowly then."

So Vern hopped into the truck bed, and to his amazement, the pig not only followed him in, but it actually looked relieved to have a welcoming face there. It nuzzled up close to him, rubbing its head against his legs and making a snuffling, crying sound. Vern's heart melted. He reached down and scratched the pig between its ears. The pig moved closer and nuzzled his knee. This pig was obviously someone's pet. How could they have so cruelly abandoned it?

Vern called me on the phone. "Hey, babe, you want a pig?"

"Huh?"

RANGER VERN WITH OUR DOG, 'TRUMAN'

"A potbellied pig. Someone left it here at Miner's Bar. Shall we try and keep it?"

"I love pigs, but you know we can't," I replied. "We have no place to put it. Is there a nearby farm that can take it? Animal control must have some connections to nearby farmers and ranchers. There are mini farms all over the area."

"Okay, hon. Thanks for the ideas. Not sure what we'll do. Wish me luck!"

"Hug the pig for me!" I was almost in tears hearing the story of this poor animal. I hoped they would find a new home nearby.

Vern asked the animal control officer to drive them to the holding facility while he rode in the back with the pig. As soon as Vern sat down in the bed of the truck, the pig lay down and nestled up against his legs. He patted it on the head the whole way there.

Happily enough, the pig was adopted the following week by a local rancher who was thrilled to have it.

"So, was it a boy or a girl?" I asked Vern later, when he got home.

"It was a pig!"

"Yes, but what was it?"

"Dunno," he said. "It was a nice one, though!"

10.
ATTACK OF THE
KILLER CATERPILLARS

Sometimes nature throws a real curve ball at us. Crazy and unexpected things can happen that simply defy logic. In 1986 there was a caterpillar plague that shrouded the Sierra Nevada foothills region in sticky, alien webbing. It was frightening.

Every tree, especially oak trees, were covered with thick, yellow, translucent curtains of caterpillar silk. Luminous sticky sheets twenty to thirty feet tall shimmered in the air, covering trees, fences, picnic tables, and camping vehicles like a creepy, shrouded invader. It was everywhere, thick veils with caterpillars attached to them by the millions. It was like a vision from a horror movie: a bug-infested hell.

"Why don't you rangers do something about this?" an elderly park visitor grumbled at me. "We made camping reservations months ago to stay here. The least you rangers could do is clean this stuff out of the trees! We are taxpayers, you know!"

This older, heavy-set man was clearly distraught as he peeled off layers of the stuff from himself, his tent, and all over his camping gear. There was no escaping it.

"I'm sorry, sir. What you're experiencing are oak worms, and this is all just a part of nature," I told him.

"Nature? Like hell! This looks like an alien invasion! Can't you take a broom and sweep it down at least?"

"We're working on it, sir, but it has us stumped. We've never seen anything of this magnitude before."

I left in a hurry because something about his angry scowl, his gruff demeanor, his puzzled attitude, and the whole ridiculous situation made me want to laugh out loud. What did he expect us to do, come out with a colossal vacuum cleaner and suck up all the webs? This was a force of nature to be reckoned with. I wondered how often something of this magnitude happened. I'd never seen or heard of anything like it in my life, and I was thirty-two years old at the time.

What exactly caused this phenomenon? A variety of different caterpillar species populate a tree by laying their eggs in the bark or on the underside of the leaves. The caterpillars hatch into larvae and consume the tree leaves. Oak worms, gypsy moths, tent caterpillars, leaf worms and other little bugs spin a silky substance which, in great enough quantities, can completely envelop a tree, sheltering the grubs as they consume the foliage. Most oak trees survive minor onslaughts just fine, but a full-blown infestation like this one could defoliate and kill a tree, or an entire forest.

That year, for some reason, an explosion of caterpillars hatched. Perhaps it was the huge rainfall that spring. Or the increasingly warmer temperatures, or both. Who knew? But it *was* frightening. Campers left the park in droves, their cars and trailers covered with the ghostly yellow webs. Even the surrounding neighborhoods were covered with the sticky stuff. I phoned Placer County Environmental Health and asked them about the issue.

"What can be done to control this weird infestation? I understand it is a natural occurrence, but this seems extreme."

"We know. It's a natural cycle of unnatural proportions. We have to deal with it quickly or these bugs will deforest the entire region. We're working on a spray that contains parasitic wasps to hunt, attack, and kill the caterpillars. We plan to spray it all over the region at no cost to the residents."

"How will you accomplish this?" I asked.

"We come around in tanker trucks with big spraying rigs and soak all the vegetation with it. It won't harm anyone, but it will knock the caterpillar population back down to normal levels."

"Is it toxic to humans? Will we have billions of wasps flying around afterward?"

"No, ma'am. The wasps paralyze the caterpillars and lay their eggs inside them. When the eggs hatch, the young wasps consume the caterpillars. These wasps are very small and don't sting like their much larger cousins, so you don't need to worry. We will be out in a few days to do the spraying."

It sounded like some kind of sci-fi horror movie: *Killer Bees vs. Mothra.*

However, the county staff delivered. The following week, tanker trucks were everywhere, spraying down everything. It was a war on caterpillars. *Attack! Attack! Attack!* Within two weeks, the infestation miraculously cleared up. The thick, goopy curtains fell to the ground in shreds, with the shattered remains of our tiny attackers still stitched into the now innocuous webbing. Their tiny little corpses morphed into dry husks. By the end of the following week, all traces of them disappeared like a bad dream, webbing and all. We were intensely grateful that the war had ended.

Good riddance!

Of course, there were always different kinds of wildlife on display ...

11.

LOVE ON THE ROCKS

One summer day I was patrolling around Oak Point at the north end of Granite Bay with another ranger named Mick. It was hot outside, and we were tired of breaking up fights at Main Granite Beach.

Suddenly, Mick told me, "Stop the car and pullover there!"

"What?" I asked, as I pulled to the curb.

"Will you look at that?" Mick said.

"What?" I asked. "Look at what?"

"There! Right over there!"

We got out of the car and walked to the side of the road. I looked over to where Mick was pointing. About one hundred feet away there was a young couple lying in the sand between some rocks and boulders. They were out of view of anyone down at the beach, and didn't realize they could be seen from the road above. They looked to be in their teens: a young brunette girl and a slim, dark-haired young man. They were completely naked, coupling with each other, and totally oblivious to the world around them.

"Oh, I see what you mean," I said, wondering how in the heck we should approach this situation.

"Should I shout at them to desist on the car PA system?" I asked Mick. "That will shake them up and stop their lurid behavior."

"No, we don't want to give them a heart attack. They must think they are in a secluded spot where no one can see them. How about if we just walk quietly up to them and suggest they get a room?"

"Jeez, Mick, I feel so embarrassed."

"Why? People do this all the time, you know."

I laughed. "Yes, but generally not in plain view of others!"

"They probably have no idea that they are in plain sight from the road. We need to let them know they have to relocate."

That's putting it mildly, I thought. Ah, the questionable joys of being a park ranger.

"What will we say to them?"

"I think they'll stop when they see us."

Uh-huh, I thought. They didn't seem to notice anyone but each other. We got within two feet of them and still no one noticed the two park rangers towering over them.

"Uh, excuse me," I finally said. Still no response. "Hello, State Park Rangers!" I said in a louder voice.

The girl was on the bottom with her eyes closed. She heard my voice and opened them in total alarm. She tapped her boyfriend on the back, but he remained oblivious to the situation.

"Stop what you're doing!" Mick finally said in exasperation.

Both youngsters jumped up in total shock.

"We're sorry! We'll never do it again!" they pleaded.

"Somehow, I doubt that," Mick replied. "Do you have any identification?"

"Uh, yeah," they both muttered.

"Put your clothes on and we'll talk," he told them.

We identified them and found them both to be minors. Just two dopey kids who thought they were alone and out of view from their group of friends.

"Are you gonna take us to jail?" the young man asked, shaking with apprehension. The young woman started to cry softly at the prospect.

"No," I said. "You didn't know you were in view of others. Next time, just be more aware of your surroundings before you decide to share your affections."

I kind of felt bad for them. They kept saying "We'll never do it again!"

"Don't make promises you can't keep." Mick smiled, and we let them go.

We laughed all the way back to the office. Those poor kids! They probably still remember those moments today, decades later.

Breaking up the naked romantic encounters of teenagers in public view was just one of the many duties park rangers performed.

12.
"CAN I SEE YOUR FISHING LICENSE, PLEASE?"

For those who like to fish, it's a joy to catch a gleaming rainbow trout or a nice, juicy bass. But, of course, many places require a fishing license. Beal's Point at Folsom Lake was a very popular spot for fishermen. A lot of people liked to fish there from the shore when the lake level was low, because they could drive right down to the water's edge. Silty, blue water sparkled in the sunlight, and fishermen sat out in folding chairs looking pleased with themselves. Hot coffee and sandwiches were perched next to them on little folding tables, giving an air of happy tranquility to the scene.

I made a point of periodically checking fishing licenses, but I didn't enjoy doing this. Inevitably, I'd catch someone fishing without a license and I'd have to write them a ticket and upset their happy experience at the lake. But I got a big kick out of my husband's story.

One day, Ranger Vern decided it was time to check fishing licenses at Beal's Point. It was late autumn and it had been awhile since anyone conducted a check. He figured it was a very fine day to do this. It would give him a chance to get out of the truck and talk to people. He put on a friendly smile and sauntered over to the first little group at the water's edge.

"Good afternoon. Howya doin? Having any luck?"

"Hi, Ranger. No, they don't seem to be biting much today."

"That's a shame! Hardly makes the cost of a fishing license worthwhile when you can't at least catch a few fish."

"You got that right, Ranger!"

"Mind if I have a look at it anyhow?"

"What, the fish? We haven't caught one yet."

"No, I mean your fishing license. Mind if I see it? We need to make sure people are complying with park rules and regulations." He smiled. "It costs the state money to stock the lake with fish, and the license fee helps to cover the costs of fish hatchery management."

"Uh, the fishing pole belongs to my boy here. He's just a kid. He doesn't need a license to fish, does he?"

"No, your boy is fine. But you need a license to fish. You had two poles in the water."

"Only one pole here, Ranger."

"Sir, I took the liberty of looking through my binoculars before I drove down here, and I clearly saw you with two poles. One of them was in your hands. You wanna lift up that blanket there and let me see the pole you hid?"

"Nope. I know my rights."

"Well then, I guess we'll just proceed with the citation. I was going to let you off with a warning, but lying to a peace officer is a more serious offense."

"Billy, lift up the blanket! Well, whaddya know! I forgot about that other pole under there, heh heh heh," he lied.

"I'll need to see your driver's license and fishing license, sir."

"Here's my driver's license."

"Hmm, it looks expired."

"No waaay!"

"Yes. Can I see your fishing license?"

"Ain't got one."

As Ranger Vern wrote the ticket, all heads turned in their direction. Suddenly there was a mass exodus of trucks, cars, and vans from the beach. Clouds of dust swirled in the air as the crowd of illegal fishermen scrambled to get away. What no one realized was that Ranger Vern had kept track of the vehicles that were there in the first place. He had a long list. When his favorite patrons came back the next week, figuring *the darn ranger* was done with checking for fishing licenses, he made a bee line straight for them.

"Saw you here last week," he said. "Didn't get a chance to talk with you then and check your fishing license. But here we are again, together at last. Mind if I take a look at it now?"

"What, the pole?"

"No, sir, your fishing license."

"It was right here a minute ago; not sure where it went."

"Uh-huh. Sir, you are required by law to display your license on your person where it can be seen. But if you can find it nearby, that will be fine. Where is it?"

"Uh, I can't find it."

"Okay. May I see your driver's license please, sir?"

"Not sure where I put that either."

"That's okay. If you don't have a fishing license and you can't identify yourself, I'm unable to write you a ticket."

"Sounds fine to me, Ranger!" The crafty fisherman was smirking.

"So that means I have no other option than to take you to jail."

"What? Jail? Just 'cuz I don't have a license?"

"Because you have committed a crime by fishing without a license, and you apparently have no means to identify yourself. A citation is a written promise to appear in court. If you have no means of identifying yourself, then no citation can be written. Which leaves me no other option but to haul you to jail and have your vehicle towed out of this park. Now, I'm sure you don't want that, do you?"

"Uh, I think my driver's license is in my truck. Yep, here it is, Ranger!"

As Ranger Vern commenced to write the ticket there was once again a rapid exodus of vehicles from the area, this time even faster than before. Miraculously, all future fishermen had fishing licenses following this incident. Word travels fast in ranger land.

Although checking fishing licenses was an expected part of the ranger job, some unexpected tasks fell into the "other duties as assigned" category.

13.

JUNK CART BLUES

One day the park staff asked me if I could help them out by taking several large bags of "lost and found" items to the local thrift store in downtown Auburn. These items had been stored in the park for years with no one to claim them, so the staff located a thrift shop that was willing to accept the donation.

"Could you please take these things to the shop in Auburn? They are taking up too much space here and every single one of these items has been in storage for at least five years. Time to get rid of them."

"Sure," I said.

No big deal, I thought. How much trouble could it be? Yikes, if I'd only known what I was getting myself into that afternoon!

They trundled the bags into my car. So much stuff! Bags and bags of stuff.

"Holy smokes, how much stuff is there?" I asked in alarm. This wasn't just a few things; it was a major haul!

"How am I supposed to unload all this junk when I get there?" I asked with trepidation.

"We called ahead, and they promised to have someone there to help."

"Okay," I said doubtfully.

Jeez, it almost felt like a setup. The things a ranger has to do! It fell under the final phrase of our job description, "... other duties as required." Those "other duties" could range from greeting the Queen of England at Sutter's Fort to hauling junk to the local thrift shop.

I grumbled my acquiescence.

"Hey, don't complain! You're not the poor fool who had to accept and catalog all these darn things as they came in everyday!" they told me. "The least you can do is help us donate the stuff."

"From now on, let's not catalog anything. Just keep it for a week and then toss the junk out," I replied. No one ever came back looking for their stuff. To me, it seemed pointless.

As I drove across town it occurred to me to take the whole load straight to the dump, but then I remembered that the staff called ahead, and they were likely to track me down if I tried to pull a fast one on them. Damn!

So, here I was, stuck with worthless junk I had to deliver.

I pulled on a grubby-looking, bulky sweater I kept in my car. I didn't want to be seen in public wearing my uniform when I was outside of the park. As it turned out, this was definitely the wrong decision! The color and shape of the garment made me look like a grimy drifter. The closest parking spot near the thrift shop was a block away. I left the bags in the car and walked over. At that time, the shop was located in downtown Auburn on the corner of a busy intersection. I strolled inside and introduced myself. I guess I must have looked pretty darn grubby, because they gaped at me in alarm.

"Hello. I'm here to deliver the lost and found items the park staff called you about. Can someone please help me get them from my car in the parking lot around the corner? There are several big bags of things."

"We can't leave the front counter. That would expose the shop to theft."

I looked around. Why would anyone want to steal anything from this place, I wondered? It was a dusty, unappealing, foul-smelling, dirty, and disorganized array of cast-offs that nobody wanted. *If I were in charge I would clean this mess up,* I thought. Or clean it all out and start over.

"My staff told me they called ahead to you, and that someone would help me carry the bags in."

"Take this shopping cart to your car and you can roll it all back here."

I could see them snickering at me when they thought I wasn't looking. *What the heck?* I wondered. But then I realized that I did look disheveled after my long day at work. The moth-infested, puke-colored sweater I wore added to my look of total disarray. I had serious "hat hair" from wearing my ranger hat all day, I was exhausted, and I probably looked pretty darn comical. I could hardly blame them for thinking ill of me. I caught a glimpse of myself in a nearby mirror and confirmed my self-diagnosis: yep, pretty crummy-looking.

Once again, I thought of going to the dump. I already felt plenty dumpy. I also thought of doing a drive-by drop-off on their corner. All I needed to do was toss the bags onto the sidewalk in front of the shop. But then I could be charged with littering. After all, the police station was only a block away.

I grabbed the rusty-looking, squeaky, clunky old shopping cart that was probably stolen from the local Safeway market years before.

As I pushed the creaking hulk down the street toward my car, I felt way too conspicuous.

I reached my car and loaded all the giant plastic bags of junk into the cart. It was heavy, and as I pushed it back up the street toward the shop I leaned forward, slumping low over the cart handle, groaning with the exertion. As I looked over to my right, I saw a police car approaching. Those officers were looking me over! They visibly slowed down and one officer was clearly calling in my description on the radio! I was going to be detained, arrested, or who knows what for my disorderly appearance downtown! This would be laughable, I thought, except that those officers looked serious. I could end up in the back of a police car before I was able to properly identify myself!

I kicked it up a notch and raced the cart into the thrift store.

"Here you go!" I shouted as I ran for the door. I didn't take time to unload the cart because I could see the police car parking across the street and one of the officers getting out, ready to head my way.

"Don't you want a receipt?" they asked me.

"Keep it!" I shouted as I sprinted out the door, around the corner, and back to the safety of my car. I did not want to have to explain myself to those police officers.

Darn those guys at the office, I thought.

14.

MINERS, PROSPECTORS, AND MULES

The river confluence below Auburn was once a large open encampment. In the 1970s and early 1980s, people were allowed to camp for up to thirty days at a time. It was not unlike the Wild West down there. Shootings, campfires, death threats, drinking, and drunkenness were constant. I can speak from experience, because I had the bad sense to camp there one night, just to see what happened after dark. Gunfire and shouting kept me awake all night. Other campers, particularly the men, were leering at me as I stepped out of my sleeping bag the next morning. I left quickly.

Some of the campers were gold miners. The Mining Law of 1872 declared all mineral deposits in the United States to be free and open to exploration. Since this was public land, miners filed dredge permits, and they set up encampments along the river for miles upstream. A dredge is a large suction device on a raft that pulls up river sediments and runs them across a sluice box to recover gold. Dredges make a very noisy clatter and muddy up the river.

There must have been a hundred people camping at the confluence at any one time. The low rumbling whine of the unsightly dredge rigs could be heard echoing off the river canyon walls. The camps were generally unsanitary, and most of the miners were an unkempt lot. Many of them drank all day long while their rigs churned up the river bottom in search of gold. When the winter rains arrived, it was like a giant toilet flushing and sweeping the area clean again ... for a while.

"It's 1988, not 1888! And mining law doesn't apply here anymore!" the park rangers told the miners.

"The hell you say!" the miners would counter back. "The Mining Law of 1872 gives us the right to be here!"

They knew mining law and wore it like a badge of courage. They also knew the park rules and regulations when it came to the length of camp stays.

"You rangers got no right to evict us. We get to stay thirty days!"

"Clean up this mess and pay your camping fees right now, or you'll be leaving today," the rangers told them.

Each miner fought for the best spot on the river. The cast of characters was eye-opening, and the park rangers made up their own names for each of them.

The Fly King was a huge, bearded man. He must have weighed close to three hundred pounds. He wore filthy overalls and was covered with dirt. He was adorned with his own personal cloud of flies that swirled around him wherever he went. When he came walking past, people didn't need any urging to step aside. He wore an angry scowl as he checked out the other claims, grumbling as his giant feet trod across rocks and sand. His belly fat rolled as he rumbled along. He'd walk right up to the river, but never seemed to actually step in. Everyone wished he would, if only to dispel the flies, even for a moment. He smelled terrible. Sure, he would put his hands in the water to tend to his equipment, but that was about it.

Then there was Raven Van Skelter, the river snitch. Gaunt and hollow-eyed, he wore a ragged tie-dye shirt and torn shorts. His blond hair hung in sad ringlets, with bald patches on his scalp where scabs had fallen away. Raven always had the latest news on what was happening at the river.

"See that guy over there, the one with the long beard? He's got warrants out for his arrest! I heard him braggin' about his rap sheet (criminal history record) yesterday. That devil's done a heap of crimes a mile long, I tell ya!"

Raven was always hoping he could trade news for a better spot on the river. "If'n I tell you some more, cain't yew rangers give me some free nights so's I don't hafta pay fer a while? An honest miner kin only afford so much; it's rough tryin' to make a livin' down here!"

Dirk the Dagger Man looked especially scary. He wore a long, shiny hunting knife on his belt and could kill any challenger with a look. He wore a big, floppy felt hat; dirty, white long johns; a thick, leather belt; and black boots. His baleful glare seemed to say, "Come within ten feet of me and I'll bury this blade straight into your backside!"

Nobody wanted to get him riled. In fact, the entire camp seemed to be armed to the teeth. Everyone wore a gun, and many of them sported all kinds of weapons.

The camp women were equally interesting. Frying Pan Frannie wore an ancient housedress with faded flowers. She had sun-blistered skin, and her dishwater hair poked listlessly out from under her tired straw hat. Her faded blue eyes looked menacing as she fixed us with her stony gaze.

"Watcha want with us?" she demanded. "Somebody done somethin' wrong? Why don't you damn fools clear outta here?"

Smiling Lil and Whiskey Bill were a bit friendlier: "C'mon over and get yerself a biscuit, Rangers! We jest baked some this mornin'!"

They had a cast-iron Dutch oven buried in the ground, surrounded by hot coals. Woe to the unobservant camper who didn't watch where they were walking; an errant step could lead to a hot foot in a minute! Greasy Larry liked hanging around their campfire, and his beard showed telltale signs of whatever he'd been feasting on.

Years later, the thirty-day stay was reduced to a three-day stay, and gradually, all camping on the beach was prohibited. It took years for this to happen, though.

Some miners were more enterprising than others. There was a group camped on the Middle Fork at the base of Volcanoville Road near Georgetown. They'd somehow managed to bump and drag a teardrop trailer all the way down to the river. They also trucked down beds, dressers, cupboards, kitchen sinks, rugs, sofas, recliner chairs, and water storage tanks, all of which were scattered around outside. Several canvas tents completed the array. *Outdoor Living*, it was; *Better Homes and Gardens* it was not. But this group, at least, had manners. Their camp king, a gray-haired, older fellow with a white beard, had a courtly way about him.

"Good morning, Ranger. Come on over and have a cup of coffee. Don't be afraid, we bathe here and wash our clothes; see 'em hanging on the line over there? Our sinks are scrubbed, and we carry out all our trash."

I had to admit, their camp looked decent.

"How in the heck did you manage to drag that trailer and all this stuff down that bumpy, pothole-ridden, non-road?" I asked in wonder. "I couldn't even get my four-wheel drive truck down here when I tried last month."

"Ahh, Ranger. You don't know Jed! His family's been comin' down here for fifty years!" one of the other miners chirped with a toothy grin.

"Is that how long this trailer has been here?"

"Nope, jest brought this one down last week. This is the *new* one!"

Good grief, I thought. Still, they all seemed nice enough and I enjoyed their company. I stayed and talked with them awhile and got all the latest news on the river. It was a great way to learn what the locals were up to, including the boaters.

But our all-time favorite was a miner named Clyde who lived at the edge of Cherokee Bar, off Sliger Mine Road. He was a character. A nineteenth century miner living in the twentieth century, with his main mode of transportation being a mule by the name of Clem. Sometimes I envied his easygoing lifestyle.

Clyde was tall and slim, with reddish-blond hair and a beard. Some days he wore only his blue overalls. Other days, he might sport a checkered shirt and a neck scarf if he was feeling fancy. He didn't talk to people much, unless he was in a brawl at the local bar. Clem was a dark brown, agreeable mule with long, floppy ears.

Clyde used to ride his mule all the way into Georgetown (about fifteen miles) to pick up supplies, throwing gunny sacks over Clem's back so he could carry the supplies home to his camp. We'd sometimes see him ambling along the road with a serene look on his face. All was right with the world: he had found enough gold to buy a few beers at the Georgetown Hotel, dinner at the Royal Dragon Chinese Restaurant just around the corner, and enough provisions for a whole week! He'd lean way back in the saddle like he was riding a recliner chair. Clem wore a bewildered expression, as if to say, "What next?" But he knew the way to and from camp, so it didn't really matter.

We'd know when Clyde was in town because we could see Clem tied up in front of various establishments. Sometimes Clem would be waiting outside the Chinese restaurant. Clyde really enjoyed the all-you-can-eat buffet there, and we'd see Clem peering in the windows, trying to discern what was happening inside, and wondering in anticipation when his buddy would come back out again.

Later on, Clem would be tied up in front of the Georgetown Hotel Saloon, while Clyde went inside to "partake of the waters." Clyde would have brought Clem right inside that saloon if he was allowed. The two of them were inseparable. As wild as that place was then, and still is today, it's a wonder that mules *aren't* allowed inside.

Clyde was barred from entering the Miner's Club saloon at the east end of town, though. Apparently, he got himself into some serious brawls there. Each miner who frequented the saloon had bragging rights to their claims. Sometimes Clyde tried to dispute claim boundaries, and this got him thrown out onto the street.

Clyde had quite a camp set up, with a claptrap cabin made from scraps of wood. Some pieces were old boards he found on the ground; other pieces were bits of river driftwood that had tumbled downstream. All of it was tied together with twine. Inside, the front room doubled as a tack room, with Clem's bridle and saddle hanging from the walls. A creaky metal bed stood in the corner topped with a decrepit cotton ticking mattress. An old wool blanket sat folded on top. A beat-up rocking chair sat next to the little wood stove in the center of the room. It looked almost cozy in a disheveled sort of way.

Outside was a makeshift kitchen with a piece of plywood on top of two sawhorses topped with an ancient Coleman gas stove, which looked like it hadn't been cleaned in twenty years. Clyde mostly ate out of his plastic gold pan and drank from his metal enamelware cup. He kept a spoon tied to his belt and a pocketknife in the leather pouch around his waist.

The view from the cabin was serenely beautiful, looking out across the pine-covered canyon. The deep blue river coursed down the straight, two mile-long channel from Cherokee Bar to Poverty Bar before it turned sharply west again.

Clyde had a corral for Clem which he'd constructed out of sawed-up pine trees lashed together. Clem didn't mind being kept in the corral as long as he was fed and given water. He liked hearing the echoes of his braying bouncing back to him from the canyon walls. To a mule, this is the sweetest music in the world.

Clyde had no car because he was a drinker. Sober, he was a gentleman. Drunk, he was a wild man. He had a long history of being drunk and disorderly in public. If he had to drive anywhere, he would end up at the local jail.

One day, a woman deputy asked Ranger Vern to accompany her as she went in to arrest Clyde. He had warrants out for failure to appear on various charges.

When the officers arrived, Clyde was cooking breakfast.

"Can I do a couple of eggs for you guys?"

"Thanks, anyway, partner. We're sorry, but we need to take you to jail for outstanding warrants."

"You want some coffee?" Clyde held out two gray enamelware cups with hot coffee in each. "I know'd you was a comin'," he continued. "I woulda taken care of those charges, ma'am, but that means a trip to Placerville at the county seat. That's about forty-nine miles round trip from here, and it's a heck of a long way to go on a mule! Ain't got no use for a car, as you can see."

When they searched the cabin, the officers found prospecting tools hung from hooks on the walls and weapons everywhere, including handguns and rifles under the bed.

"This rifle is fer mountain lions, that one's fer shootin' rattlesnakes, and the shotgun is fer coyotes. I gotta protect Clem," Clyde said.

For the most part, the camp was benign, and the miner was no real threat to anyone. It seemed almost a shame to haul him away.

Clyde quietly accepted his fate of being arrested. He knew he had escaped "the law" for a long, long time. His biggest concern was for Clem.

"Is somebody going to feed my mule?"

The deputy promised that county animal control would come get Clem and take him to a new home if the miner didn't return. Ranger Vern promised to drop off some feed for Clem in the meantime.

As they began the long walk back to the patrol car, Clyde looked back over his shoulder at his beloved camp. He hollered to Clem, "Bye, old friend. You behave yerself!"

Not all rough and tumble guys were prospectors. Some were just out for the day, racing recklessly down the road.

15.

THE SCREAMING DAD

One Father's Day a wild man was tearing down the road on the way to Beal's Point, a popular campground and day-use area at Folsom Lake. He was swerving onto the road shoulder, kicking up dirt, and then swerving into the oncoming traffic lane at high speed. He was clearly going to hurt someone. I put on the red lights, but he didn't seem to notice. He raced ahead and then roared into his campsite, coming to a screeching halt in a big cloud of dust. When he finally saw me, he leaped out of his truck, screaming and hollering.

"What the hell are you doing? I done nothin' wrong!"

He was stomping around in circles, waving his arms in the air. His wife and two young boys piled out of the truck, dumbfounded by his behavior, and just stared at him in alarm. He held a beer bottle in his right hand, shaking it at me in outrage.

"You got no right to bother me! Don't you know this is Father's Day? This is a family day! We are out here having our family time and now you are ruining it!"

"Sir," I said calmly, "I need to see your license and registration, please. You were driving at a high rate of speed and swerving all over the road. I stopped you because you are posing a danger to yourself and others."

The guy was obese and wore brown shorts, a black T-shirt, and a baseball cap screwed on backward. He clomped around in brown boots.

"You can't do this! I'm here with my family! This is Father's Day! Leave us alone!"

"Sir, your behavior is erratic and combative. Please settle down."

The man's wife handed me his license and registration while the two little boys looked on in confusion and fear. I felt terrible for them.

What must they be thinking? I wondered. *Poor little kids!* I felt badly that they were witnessing such a spectacle.

I wrote him a ticket for speeding and for having an open container of alcohol in a vehicle. I checked him to make sure he wasn't driving under the influence. Nope, he was just an idiot. A sober idiot.

He continued to holler and stomp around, shouting about the injustice, screaming that I had shamed him.

"Look how you are embarrassing me in front of my family!"

"Sir, you are embarrassing yourself. Stop your shouting. Sign this citation and we'll be done."

"I'm not signing anything, dammit!"

"Sir, signing the ticket is not an admission of guilt. It merely says that you are promising to appear in court. Failure to sign means I will have to take you into custody."

"Naw!!! I'm *not* going to jail!"

At this point his wife interjected and told him he needed to cooperate. She appealed to him to sign the ticket so this awful episode would be over. Finally, he acquiesced, grabbed the ticket book, and signed his name, muttering obscenities. His poor kids stood by mutely and watched.

"I hope you realize you've ruined our day!"

I turned to his wife and kids. "I'm really very sorry about this. He was driving so dangerously."

"Please don't feel bad; it's not your fault. He's just upset. Please just go now before he starts yelling some more," the wife said. "I'm so sorry he is acting up like this."

"Ma'am, are you and the kids alright?"

"We're fine; he is just worked up. He's had a very rough week at work. He's having trouble with his boss, and he is angry. I'll get him to calm down. Don't worry, he's a very good husband and father."

"Don't let him drive, ma'am."

"I won't, believe me."

I left somewhat reluctantly, but realized things would only get worse if I stayed.

A couple of months later I received a subpoena to the Loomis traffic court. *Oh no!* I thought. *Not this guy again!* I went to court, dreading the scene about to unfold. I thought about my strategy. But there was no need. As soon as it was time to plead his case, the man stood up and started shouting and stomping around in the courtroom.

"Your Honor, that lady ranger ruined my day! She ruined Father's Day! I was minding my own business, and she stopped our truck. Then she wrote me a ticket—in front of my whole family! She made a scene!"

"Mr. Johnson, you are the one making a scene," the judge said.

But the guy didn't seem to hear. He was too busy ranting and pacing around the courtroom.

"She yelled at us! She was out of control!" he hollered, waving his arms in a frenzy.

"Mr. Johnson, stop this behavior at once! If this is the way you behaved when Officer McHenry contacted you, I'm surprised she didn't immediately put you in handcuffs. If it were me, I would have taken you straight to jail!"

"But she had no business writing me a ticket!"

"You were driving above the speed limit and weaving all over the road. Do you deny this?"

"No, but ..."

"You endangered the lives of your own family members driving that way. You were drinking while driving. Do you deny this happened?"

"No, but she was rude to me ..."

"Mr. Johnson, I've heard enough. Your traffic fine would have been $160.00. I'm fining you $1,500 for disturbing this courtroom with your behavior!"

"Your Honor, she should never have ..."

"*Silence!* Or would you prefer thirty days in jail?"

For once, the guy shut up. His shoulders sagged. He stood there mutely. I felt badly for the guy.

"Leave this courtroom at once and go pay your fine! Officer McHenry, I'm sorry you had to deal with this person. You have far more patience than I do."

"I'm sorry, too, Your Honor."

It was the one and only time I went to court to defend a ticket and never had to say a single word to explain my actions.

16.

"I'M JUST A REDNECK COWBOY, AND I'M DRUNK OFF MY ASS!"

We all have imagined the classic Hollywood drunk careening down the roadway, weaving wildly to the left and right, and eventually crashing into a tree. Well, one day I actually met this classic drunk at a busy intersection on Auburn Folsom Road.

I told him on the loudspeaker to pull over. He spasmodically jerked his car over to the left road shoulder, through the oncoming traffic lane, and crashed up onto the sidewalk. Then his car shuddered to a stop. The driver's door swung open, and a bottle of whiskey flew through the air, crashing to the ground. The bottle rolled about ten feet, then wobbled to a rest, lying there like a stunned corpse. As if this wasn't entertaining enough, the driver then spilled out of the car onto the sidewalk, flopping onto his back while laughing his head off.

I pulled my patrol car over and walked carefully toward him. He was muttering something, and as I got closer, he shouted:

"I'm just a redneck cowboy, and I'm drunk off my ass!"

What the heck? I wondered.

"I'm just a redneck cowboy, and I'm drunk off my ass!!!" Then he began to laugh even louder. He wore a red bandanna tied around his neck, a blue checkered cowboy shirt, dusty blue jeans, and brown, two-toned cowboy boots. His dirty blond hair fell across his sunburned face as he laughed and shouted even louder, *"I'm just a redneck cowboy, and I'm drunk off my ass!"*

I looked around for the candid camera and tried very hard not to laugh out loud at this ridiculous scene. What a cliché! It was like something out of a movie. The red bandana around his neck was the funniest part. He looked like a burned-out desperado.

"Hey, buddy, just how much have you had to drink?" I asked him.

He laughed even louder and then pointed to the whiskey bottle.

"I've done drunk most of that thing!" he happily exclaimed, then rolled over onto his stomach and vomited.

He must have been telling the truth, because the bottle was nearly empty. If I'd drunk even half that much, I'd be dead on delivery.

"Well, I'm really sorry, buddy, but you know I'm going to have to arrest you and take you to jail. You understand that, don't you?"

"Sure thing, Ranger Lady. You go ahead, 'cause I'm just a redneck cowboy."

"And you're drunk off your ass. Yep, I got that message earlier," I told him.

Where did this dude come from? I wondered. He could have killed someone driving like that, but he didn't seem to care. So, I strolled over and put handcuffs on him, taking care not to hurt him. He just laughed even louder and threw up again. I rolled him onto his side. He was kind of funny and even likable in a ridiculous way. At least he was expelling all the hooch out of his gut.

As we drove to the jail, he asked three times if I would stop so he could duck his head out of the car and throw up again. Normally, I would have been alarmed, but he was very entertaining the way he retched, laughed, and retched again. I stood next to him in case he passed out, but somehow, he remained conscious. I wondered if he was like this when he was sober. If he was ever sober, that is.

"What is so darn funny?" I asked.

"Hell, lady! Life is funny! You outta try it sometime!"

"What, drinking?"

"No, *living!* You look like you got a big ole stick up your butt, sister!"

"Well, I imagine that's pretty close to the truth, buddy!" (His assessment of me was funny, I had to admit.)

By the time we got to the jail, he had passed out completely, snoring loudly, farting, muttering, and laughing in his sleep. I called ahead to tell the jail deputies that we would need to carry this one into the drunk tank. Three of them met me as I drove up to the gate.

"Looks like a redneck!" the lead deputy jokingly said.

"Yep." I answered.

The deputies carried him into the jail and booked him into the drunk tank: a large holding cell for drunks where they can cool their heels until they're safe to leave.

The "cowboy" dude had no identification of any kind. There was nothing in his car to indicate where he came from except for a long-outdated registration form in the glove box. I ran the car license plate, but it came back as registered to someone who was deceased. *Where did this guy come from?* I wondered.

So, he was booked as a John Doe, pending further identification. A week later I called the jail to inquire about his status.

"He's still here," the deputy told me. "We still don't know who he is, and he can't seem to remember. I think he just likes the food here, or maybe he likes the accommodations. We run a pretty decent jail."

"You mean to tell me no one can find out who this guy is?"

"Nope. You book 'em and we cook 'em. We keep them for as long as it takes to figure it out. Let us know if you figure it out."

I called back two weeks later. It had been a very busy month. When I spoke to the jail deputy, the story was the same as before: no one knew who the cowboy was, nor did they have any idea where he hailed from.

"Why didn't you just release him?" I asked. "I brought him to jail to get him off the streets so he wouldn't harm anyone while he was drunk."

"Well, we need to know who he is before we can let him go. Of course, you could always come to the jail and write a release form for him, but since there is no way to tell who this person is, you would have to accept responsibility for him. You can come in and interview him if you like."

"I'll check back later," I replied. I kept hoping someone would come claim him and take him off our hands. Two months passed, and still no one knew who the cowboy dude was. I went and interviewed him, but this yielded no results. He just acted like he didn't understand anything. He had become friends with all the local inmates. The jailers were beginning to think of him as family. He sat in his cell telling stories about life on some ranch. He laughed a lot and kept the other inmates in good spirits.

Finally one day, a distant cousin arrived at the jail to identify the mystery dude. It seemed our "cowboy" came all the way from Alabama on some sort of bender after he was fired from his job. He didn't seem to care where life took him.

"Now that we know who he is, do you want to go forward with the DA's office and set a court date with the judge to file charges?" the deputy asked me.

"Let him go," I said. "He's served enough time as it is. Besides, he's cost the taxpayers of California far too much money already. Hopefully, he has learned a valuable lesson."

"The only lesson this fool has learned is that California is the best state in the union to get arrested in. He has been eating well, sleeping well, and will probably be back again, considering the treatment he has received."

"Good grief," I said. "Just let him go. Have his cousin take him home to Alabama."

"We're gonna miss him around here," the deputy said, almost wistfully.

And that was the last any of us saw of that cowboy. I think they still talk about him at the jail all these years later.

The cowboy's drunk driving caused me to stop him that day, but sometimes park visitors are stopped by their own crazy driving.

17.

MUDSLINGERS

Starlight, star bright, I wonder what's in store tonight? I thought to myself. There is that divine moment between sunset and twilight when everything is peaceful and beautiful. The setting sun casts lengthened shadows across the landscape. The lake is silent and still. *Ahhh, this is why I love being a park ranger, to enjoy the outdoors like this,* I thought.

Until the idiots arrive for the night.

During the winter at Folsom Lake, when the lake level drops way down, the blue water recedes, leaving behind lots of sticky, gray, goopy mud. At these times, the strangest people come out to drive their four-wheel drive trucks through the sludge. They bob and weave, crashing and bashing, up and down ravines, in and out of puddles, and through slimy pools. They race back and forth, splattered in mud, until they eventually roll their Jeeps over, or get stuck in the mud and call for rescue. I couldn't understand the joy in this. To me, it seemed disgusting to get covered in grime. Ugh!

For some reason, these people usually waited to call for help until long after sunset when the ranger was driving around, trying to close the park gates. Every night, the rangers would call out on the loudspeaker while closing the park: "The park will be closing in thirty minutes. Please proceed to the park entrance now."

And again, fifteen minutes later: "The park will be closing in fifteen minutes. Please proceed to the front gate to depart."

Then finally: "The park is now closed. Anyone remaining in the park after closing will be cited."

"Help us! We're stuck in the mud!" People would scream from a half mile away near the lakeshore, entrenched up to their axles in mud.

"Guess your vehicle is spending the night." I would answer.

"Help us get our truck out!"

"How'd you get stuck? This isn't an off-road driving area."

"We thought it was okay."

"You drove past several signs warning you not to drive beyond that point over there, on the paved road. There are reasons the signs are there: so that you won't get stuck in the mud. Now you need to park your cars and walk out. You can call for a tow truck in the morning. No one will take them."

"We need you to call a tow truck!"

"You can call for one in the morning. The gates open at 6:00 a.m."

I had pulled countless rigs out of the mud and was tired of doing it. These people knew better than to drive down, way below lake level, crashing around and tearing up the park like it was a mud derby. I had a job to do, and there were many gates to close. My job did not include pulling trucks out of the mud. Management became very angry with staff for working overtime, so the last thing I wanted to do was get in trouble.

The next day I arrived at work to face an upset supervisor with a visitor complaint form in his hand.

"Why did you leave this group stranded?"

"You and the other supervisors constantly tell us not to rack up overtime hours. We could easily spend four hours each night towing trucks out of the mud and never get the park gates closed. What do you want us to do? Are we in the business of towing people out of the mud every night? Is this why we are out there?"

"No, of course not. You are supposed to be locking gates."

"Then why are we even discussing this?"

"Because we got this written complaint and ..."

"Excuse me, why are we even accepting written visitor complaints for this?"

"Because the superintendent wants an answer."

"With all due respect, I believe I just gave you one."

That was the last time a supervisor talked to anyone on our shift about late-night towing. They knew I was right.

The next week, though, something amazing happened to change my attitude about helping people who got stuck in the mud. My husband, Vern, told me his story about a day when he was on patrol, and *he* was the one who got stuck. Normally, he drove a four-wheel drive truck, but he was on a late shift that day. By the time he got to the truck yard, the only thing left to drive was the ancient Chevy sedan. It was a tired old hunk of junk.

"Hmmm," he wondered aloud. "Should I even try to take this thing down onto the beach? Or should I just hang out here at the ranger office, have a cup of coffee and write reports?"

He hated report writing. There would be time for that later, or maybe not at all, if he was lucky. He looked at the Dispatch Activity Log. No one had been out to Oak Point all day. It was just him and one other ranger on duty until the graveyard shift came on two hours later.

"I guess I'd better get out there and check on things," he said to no one in particular.

If someone got stuck, he didn't want to have to deal with it in the dark. But at the same time, the office seemed like such a cozy place to hang out. He looked wistfully over at the box of doughnuts next to the dispatcher station. They looked fabulous, and it was still a long way until dinnertime. When no one was watching, he grabbed a chocolate éclair and made a break for the door with keys in hand. He chomped it down on the way to the car.

"I saw that, Ranger 616!" the dispatcher's voice called on his portable radio. He ran into the sedan and roared out of the yard, laughing.

When he got out to the lakefront at Oak Point, he saw a few groups milling around near the water's edge. He didn't like driving down to the beach, even when he was driving a four-wheel drive truck. But it was winter, the lake level was low, and the shore was a quarter of a mile away from the road this time of year. It was too far to walk down there this late in the day. He put the car in drive and slowly drove out across the sand and mud. The group of guys he wanted to talk to were behaving alright. He just wanted to check on them before night fell so they didn't get stuck in the mud, like so many others seemed to do on a daily basis.

About one thousand feet out into the sand, he got stuck. The front and rear tires were completely mired in the muck. Repeated attempts to break free only caused the wheels to dig in deeper.

"Dammit, dammit, dammit!" he said aloud, banging his fists on the dashboard. He may as well be stranded on Mars. Oak Point was quite a distance out from the main entrance leading into the park.

Now he was in the embarrassing position of needing a tow for his sedan. Or, he could radio Dispatch to send someone out later with a tow line to drag it out. He didn't like either one of these options. Both were too embarrassing to contemplate, so he just sat there, ruminating, with an angry scowl on his face, as the sun dropped low in the sky. After a few moments, he heard a voice right outside his window.

"Hey Ranger, you alright?"

"Huh?" Ranger Vern said, startled from his dark reveries.

"You look upset, dude. Can we help you?"

Standing outside was a group of seven young men. They looked like a Charles Atlas review; every one of them was obviously a heavyweight lifter.

"Sure. Can you help me get this sedan out of this sand and mud? I figure we'll need to tow it about twenty feet to get me back onto more solid ground."

"Okay," they answered, and surrounded the sedan. They all reached under the car to lift it up.

"Wait, what are you guys doing? Don't you want me to get out of the car before you try to budge it? I weigh 210 pounds. Where's your tow vehicle?"

"No need," they answered.

The next thing Ranger Vern knew, he was being bodily lifted, car and all, back to a firm spot in the sand. He could hardly believe it. These men lifted and carried him at least twenty feet, and they made it look easy!

"Were you wanting to talk to us?" they asked. "We saw you heading our way before you got stuck."

"I was just going to warn you not to get stuck, but I guess I don't need to worry about that," he laughed. "Thanks for lifting me out of there!"

"No problem, Ranger. Drive safe, man."

18.
GUN-TOTING MADMAN

Sometimes I wondered, do normal people go to the park to have a nice time? Yes, they do, but unfortunately, they sometimes get threatened by dangerous whackos.

One winter day my partner Daryl and I got called to the scene of some lunatic threatening people with a gun at Granite Bay. We arrived at the main entrance and spoke to the victims.

"There's a crazy guy in a beat-up, white sedan near the beach who threatened to shoot us with a big old gun!" they said.

"Why did he threaten you? Can you describe him further? Did you get the license plate of his car?" and so on. We asked the usual questions.

"He is a maniac. We were having a quiet little picnic over by the beach and he drove up, pulled out a gun and threatened to kill us. So, we raced out of there!"

Jeez! A madman with a gun threatening people. It sounded dangerous. We radioed back the information to Dispatch, then set out looking for the perpetrator. About a half mile north we found him, racing around in his car near the launch ramp. We put the lights on him to stop. He sped up and raced around some more until he figured out that we weren't leaving, so he suddenly braked the car to a skidding halt.

He leaped out of the car yelling at us: "Whaddya doing following me? I ain't done nothin!"

"Step away from the car! Put your hands in the air!" my partner shouted at him. We had no idea if he had weapons on him.

We searched and handcuffed him, then set him down on the ground until we could safely assess the situation. We walked up to his car and immediately found a loaded handgun on the front seat near the driver's side. A quick visual search of the car revealed several boxes of handgun ammunition on the front seat, as well as a .22 rifle and more boxes of rounds on the back seat.

"I wasn't shooting at those people, if that's what you're here about," the driver hollered.

We radioed back to the park entrance station and requested that the reporting party come out to us. They made a positive identification on the driver as the person who threatened them with a gun. It was a miracle no one was injured. We did a background check on the driver and found he had countless arrests for assaulting people with deadly weapons. This was an extremely dangerous person. Later in the week we spoke with the Placer County District Attorney.

"This is an extremely dangerous subject with a long list of former arrests. He needs to be charged with Assault with a Deadly Weapon so he will get convicted of a felony and sent to prison," we pleaded with him.

"We usually plea bargain these charges down to a misdemeanor weapons display offense so we can at least obtain an admission of guilt."

"But he threatened people with a gun! Someone could have been killed. Then we would be looking at murder. This guy belongs in prison. He keeps committing the same crimes, and you guys keep pleading down the charges against him so that he is never held to answer. Someday, he is going to kill a person!"

"Be that as it may, I'm going to try and get a plea bargain."

My partner and I begged this DA. We even talked with his boss. But they were already dealing with several homicide cases and didn't have time for us. We felt completely disillusioned by the criminal justice system. Sure enough, the guy spent a few days in jail and was released on bail for a misdemeanor charge. We feared he would be back in the park or somewhere else nearby, shooting at people until there was an actual murder.

California justice! After this situation, I made it my personal mission to get to know each of the deputy district attorneys. I figured out which ones were really in charge (as opposed to the sycophants who blindly followed orders) and l hand-carried my crime reports to them in person. I made appointments to meet personally with each of them and discuss individual cases. Eventually I got to know them all, including the lead district attorney. I walked them through every point of my reports and told them exactly why the defendants were charged with crimes. I refused to take no for an answer. I sat with them at countless preliminary hearings and felony criminal trials. I sat through witness selections when cases were brought to trial. I did everything I could to help ensure that crimes committed in the park came to justice.

All too often, cases fell through the cracks because of poor report writing or fear of failure on the part of the prosecuting attorney. They each had intense pressure on them to win in court, so I did everything I could think of to make their jobs easier. Consequently, my cases usually won.

Do people sometimes get accused of crimes they didn't commit? It never happened with one of my arrests. If I took someone into custody, it was because they presented a clear and present danger to the park and the people in it. If someone behaved in a harmful manner, they were brought to justice. It was my job to protect the park and the people in it, and I took my job seriously.

19.

THE NAKED MAN

Of course, there were times when the perpetrator wasn't a criminal, but a mentally compromised individual who needed help.

One day, while I was temporarily assigned to the South Yuba River State Park near Nevada City, I came across a young man who was running buck naked in the woods. This was not an uncommon sight, as many back-to-nature enthusiasts loved swimming nude in the river and camping in the buff about a mile upstream. The area below the Highway 49 Bridge crossing on the South Yuba River was a popular swimming spot. Cool, clear water cascaded down over giant, white granite boulders, creating deep emerald pools, which shimmered in the sunlight and made stunning swimming holes. I often dreamed of jumping in myself, it looked so inviting.

Groups of teenagers loved congregating there, drinking and partying. About half a mile upstream was Pan's Pool, a popular nude swimming spot. A trail on the north side of the river connected these two points. A parking lot at the bridge provided a place to leave cars, so lots of people walked upstream and downstream from there. The problems there were ongoing. Some days it felt like utter chaos with boom boxes blaring, teenagers drinking and fighting, guns going off, threats being traded, and injuries being inflicted. Cracked skulls and broken bones were not uncommon there.

One frequent visitor there was a young man with a terrible drug problem. He was stable enough when he stayed on his antidepressants. But if he ran out of his medication, he became mentally compromised. His name was Mark, and I had seen him many times before. But this day was different.

"Respond to a case of a young man shouting and running naked along the river at Highway 49 crossing," Dispatch called us.

When my partners and I arrived, we found Mark running through the forest just upstream of the bridge. He was shouting gibberish and racing back and forth with a wild expression in his eyes. We tried to grab him, but Mark kept running away. We didn't want to hurt him. He was in top physical condition, about twenty years old. He was beautiful to look at with blue eyes, shoulder length wavy hair, and a strong, muscular, medium build. He wasn't harming anyone, but he was clearly a danger to himself. We needed to capture him and take him to the county health department before he injured himself.

I finally arrived at a solution. I walked slowly over to where Mark was feverishly pacing back and forth and sat down near him, not looking directly at him, and speaking very softly.

"Mark, I'm so sorry you feel upset today. You look thirsty. And it's so hot outside."

He stopped moving and just looked at me.

"I feel hot, so hot," I said to him. "It's so hot outside. I hate it here in this heat, don't you? Would you like some cool water? I have some in my car."

"I'm thirsty," Mark replied.

"My car is nice and cool, with air conditioning. You can come sit inside and have a cool drink of water."

He thought this over and shook his head no.

"I'm worried about you, Mark. Did you run out of your medicine?"

"Yes, I ran out. I can't remember when or how to get some more."

"Mark, if you come with me, I'll give you cold water and take you to the county center so we can get you some more medicine."

He looked warily at me. Clearly, other officers had picked him up before. In that moment, my heart went out to this kind-faced, young man. It wasn't his fault that he had a chemical imbalance in his system. It may have been caused by illegal drug use, but it could also be a form of mental illness, which could only be controlled by intervention. So many people out there were helpless, just like Mark. The county health department knew him well and had seen him many times, but they had no long-term solution for him, only pills to help mitigate his chronic condition. This saddened me greatly.

I reached out my hand to him. "Mark, please come with me. I won't hurt you. I'll give you cold water in my car and take you over to county health."

"They just wanna lock me up!" he cried.

"They just want to help you. I want to help you. Will you come with me, please, Mark?"

"Okay."

And he did. He followed me to my car. I gave him a long, cold drink from my water bottle. I let him sit quietly for a while in the air-conditioned car. I explained that we would need to restrain him with handcuffs for the journey, but that no harm would come to him. I took him to county health, where they keep patients on a seventy-two-hour mental health observation hold, long enough to get his prescriptions refilled. Later the next week I followed up with the county health officer to see if we could get a new caseworker assigned to Mark.

"We understand your concerns, officer. But we are woefully under-staffed here. We simply do not have the staff nor the room in this facility for anyone except the most violent offenders. It's a travesty."

"Isn't there something more you can do for this young man? I want to see him get the care he really needs. He is gentle, just confused."

"We are already doing everything we can."

I left there with a great sadness. I wished with all my heart that I could do something to save this young man from his mental illness. But I was powerless to change the system. Our broken and underfunded system. There were thousands more out there like Mark, many of them far more dangerous. I sighed in frustration. Mark had no family to help him. He was alone. I wished I could take him in, adopt him. I wanted to do something, anything. But this wasn't an option.

"Please take care of him as long as you can, and help him get his medication."

"We will, but we can only keep him here seventy-two hours."

I thanked them and left. How did we come to this? We should be ashamed of the fact that our mentally ill fall through the cracks in the system like this.

It's been thirty-one years and I can still see Mark clearly in my mind's eye. Where is he today? Is he alive? He would be in his early fifties now. Did someone find a way to save that gentle, young man? I often think of him and wish I could have helped him somehow, and so many others like him.

20.

"BE GOOD OR THE RANGER WILL GET YOU!"

When we were kids, our parents often told us, "Don't talk to strangers!"

We heard this all the time. Many parents taught their kids this same thing. Beware of strangers because they could be dangerous. Okay, this made sense. Kids should be cautious about who they engaged with. We taught our kids this too. When our little daughter left for school, we told her, "Watch out for cars, don't talk to strangers, and become educated." This was back in the days when we allowed our kids to walk to school, and it was a lot for a little girl to consider.

But later, when I became a park ranger, I heard people say, "Be good or the ranger will get you!"

Now why would they say this? I wondered. Was a park ranger someone to be feared? I didn't think so. But, exasperated parents, at their wits end dealing with difficult children, saw a park ranger arrive and decided to use this as a "learning" tool to scare their kids into behaving.

So, they said things like: "You see? This ranger is here because you are causing such a ruckus. You'd better behave, or she will get you!"

Upon hearing this ominous threat, the poor kid looked in my direction and regarded me in abject horror. They probably wondered what this terrible person in uniform would do to them.

I cringed.

What an awful thing to tell your kid, I'd think. But I hid my adverse reaction and asked the parent if it would be okay for me to talk with their child. The parent always answered yes, of course, because they wanted *me* to solve *their* problem with a misbehaving kid.

So, I smiled and walked up to the child, squatted down to their eye level, and said, "Hello. I'm Ranger Rose. I'm a mama too! I have little children just like you. What's your name?"

The kids stared at me with suspicion in their little eyes. But I continued undaunted and tried to guess their name.

"Is your name Billy? Clyde? William? Is it Christine? Shaniya? Blaine?"

I guessed at names and made funny faces until they laughed and told me their correct name, or their parents did. Some would be giggling by then, wondering how a ranger could be so silly.

"That's a good name," I'd say. "How old are you?"

I'd hold up my fingers. "Two? Three? Four? Are you a kid or a fox? A lion? A bear? A mouse?" And so on, as I made even sillier faces. Pretty soon the child would laugh out loud.

"You're too silly!" they'd tell me, or "Why are you so funny?"

"Mommy just wants you to be good," I'd tell them. "Rangers want you to be good too. Rangers are here to help people. We help them when they get hurt, or when they are in trouble. We also tell them about the park. Would you like to earn a Junior Ranger badge?"

Some kids would turn away and run. I guess their parents taught them to be afraid of strangers. But most kids listened and soon realized they didn't need to be frightened of rangers. Many of them wanted to learn about a ranger's job. The parents soon realized their ploy to use rangers as a "boogeyman" had backfired. Often, they'd apologize.

"We were only trying to get him/her to behave."

"I completely understand, and it's okay. But let's teach them that park rangers are here to help and protect people."

"Of course. So sorry!"

"No problem," I'd say, heading back toward my car. Mission accomplished!

Then about fifty feet away I'd hear it again from a new set of parents.

"See that, Caroline? See that ranger? If you don't stop being a bad girl, that ranger will get you!"

Oh Jeez! Now I needed to start all over again ...

One day I approached a woman who was letting her kids play in the water at the boat launch ramp at Granite Bay. I walked over to her and explained why this wasn't a safe idea.

"Ma'am, I'm sorry, but this is not a swimming area. This is a boat launch ramp. The swimming beach is just to the right over there, see it? It's a much safer place for your little children to swim in. Here, there are boats and trailers driving up and down the ramp, and your family could get injured playing in the water. Drivers backing down the ramp might not even see you. We've had accidents here where young kids were hit by moving trailers."

But this mom was on an angry streak. With claws out and teeth gnashing, she told her kids, "Kids, you see this? The ranger is telling us we have to leave, even though we are taxpaying citizens, and she is just a public servant! Ranger, you have no right to tell us where we can swim. I pay for your salary!"

This ticked me off. I was trying to protect her and her family and she responded by angrily attacking me. I walked straight up to this mom and stared at her.

"Ma'am, is this the example you want to set for your children, to disrespect authority and ignore reason when it is for your *own* protection? Everything I am telling you is for *your* protection. Are you choosing to ignore this advice?"

The woman gaped at me. Her kids stared, open-mouthed, wondering what would happen next.

"I guess you're right," she said. "You're just trying to do your job."

"Yes, I'm trying to help keep you and your kids safe, not harassing you."

"I know. I'm sorry for being rude to you. Their father wouldn't join us today and I feel nervous trying to bring the kids here alone."

"Is everything okay at home?" I asked. "Are you alright?" I realized in that moment that she was a young and struggling mom.

"Yes, we're fine. I'm just tired."

"Do you need help, ma'am?" Now I was concerned for her. Was she a victim?

"No, thank you. He's a good man, he just couldn't come today. I'm sorry for the trouble, Ranger."

"It's okay, ma'am. We are here for our park visitors. If we contact you, it's because we don't want you to get hurt."

"I understand. Thanks, Ranger."

"You have a good day, ma'am."

The woman smiled and moved her family over to the other beach. She waved goodbye.

I sighed, because I felt for her. I knew what it was like trying to manage little children on a beach outing. I also knew the challenges of managing a family while working as a park ranger.

21.
NURSING MOM

I first began working at Folsom Lake when my infant son was only four months old. This was hard on so many levels. I was a nursing mother, and it was literally painful to be away from him for long. I lived forty minutes away from work, so feeding my son during the day wasn't an option. And I wasn't ready to give up nursing. I wanted to continue for a few more months. My choices were to use a breast pump or leak into my uniform and suffer from pain and embarrassment.

I tried going into the women's room but there was only one sink and a stall. The room was small, and it was an impossible situation. This was in 1987—long before workplaces made accommodations for nursing mothers.

I couldn't just pull over in my patrol vehicle somewhere in the field. I needed a place to plug in my pump and sit with my shirt open. How the heck was I supposed to do this? There was nowhere to go. In desperation, I spoke to the Human Resources manager, Kelly. She immediately offered me the use of her office.

"You can come in here anytime you need to. If possible, I will leave, but there may be times I'll need to be in here."

"I'm so grateful! It doesn't matter if you and other women staff come in; we just need to keep the guys away."

"Let me handle that," she said.

I went to her office once a day to pump out milk. I kept it in her little office fridge so I could bring it home later. One day, the district superintendent tried to come in while I was pumping. Kelly always locked the door to keep people out while I was there.

"Why is this door locked?" he bellowed. "Let me in!"

"I'm sorry; you can't come in right now," Kelly answered.

"Why can't I come in? I need to discuss a new contract with you."

"I'll come to your office if you like," she said.

"This is ridiculous. You have no right to lock me out, I'm your manager."

"You can't come in right now …"

"But I need to discuss …"

"You can't come in because *a nursing mother* on our staff is pumping her breasts!" Kelly finally told him.

There was a long pause, and then a contrite, "Uh, okay. Sorry, ladies," as his footsteps receded in the distance. We both sighed in relief.

"Don't worry about him. I'll explain it to him later," she said kindly.

I was extremely thankful to her. Eight years earlier, in 1978, when my daughter was a five-month-old infant, I went to work at Hearst Castle. I was a Historical Guide there. I was a nursing mom then, too, and I had no possible way to bring my child to work or to pump breast milk. There was no quiet, private place to pump, so I just suffered through it all. I leaked through my shirt, so I had to wear a uniform jacket to cover this up in the ninety-degree humid heat. It was a great job, but I endured a miserable two weeks until my body finally adjusted. Anyone who has ever been a nursing mother will understand this. It can be excruciating.

Nowadays, it is much easier for women in the workplace, but back then it was like the Dark Ages. I still don't know how I lived through it all, especially on holidays.

22.
HOLIDAY BLUES

Being a park ranger means tackling tough tasks and working most holidays. Weekends too. It just went with the job. Anyone who signed up to work as a ranger understood this.

Still, there were days when I felt my heart breaking, especially on Christmas Day and Mother's Day when my kids were little. I remember one particular Mother's Day when I took a photo of my baby boy in his stroller looking expectantly out at me with his big brown eyes. My sweet little daughter was standing next to him, smiling back at me, her blonde hair shining in the sunlight. It took a Polaroid photo so I could look at it throughout the day. I still have that photo now, decades later. How could I leave and go to work? They both looked so adorable. Ah, this was definitely the hardest part of the job.

I remember many Thanksgivings and Christmases when my husband and I had to work. Often the rangers had to dispatch for each other on Christmas Day because our regular dispatchers were off duty. One Christmas Day my husband was at work, and I was at home. I kept a portable radio with me, so I could respond to him if anything was needed. Most of the time it was very quiet in the park with very few park visitors. Often on these holidays, a park ranger could get by with opening gates in the morning, doing periodic patrols during the day, and being at home in between. But on this day, I'd heard nothing for hours, so I grabbed the radio and called him.

"Ranger 616, status?"

Silence.

"Ranger 616, status report?"

Still nothing. Was I going to have to pack the kids into the van and go looking for him? Where the heck was he? Was no one else working or at least listening in?

The phone rang. It was my husband.

"Babe, I'm getting a hot dog at the 7-Eleven store in Granite Bay. What's up?"

"I was worried. You didn't answer. How come?"

"I got hungry."

"What, you're not allowed to stop and get food? Don't be silly!"

"I took my lunch break earlier, remember? But I'm hungry again."

"What did you eat earlier?"

"Doughnuts and Doritos. And a cola."

"Good grief! No wonder you're hungry. I'm surprised you didn't go into a diabetic coma eating like that. Were you asleep or something?"

"Too many questions."

"Okay, well don't disappear like that again."

"Jeez, you sound like a real dispatcher!"

"Get back to work, 616, so you can finish up soon and come home to dinner. And don't eat any more junk food!"

"Yes, ma'am!"

Later I would find candy bar wrappers and Hostess cupcake packages in the car. My husband, the hopeless junk food junkie. I knew how it was. Things often got so busy there was no time to stop and eat. As patrol rangers we often ate our meals in the car as we drove along park roads. I became quite an expert at eating and drinking at thirty miles per hour. But when I got home in the evening, it was time to cook dinner. No one else was going to do it for me. We had two young children and worked opposite shifts. Often, my husband and I would go a week before seeing each other awake.

I'd come home from work, drop my gun belt with one hand, grab my apron with the other hand, and trudge immediately to the stove to make food.

"What are we having for dinner, Mom?" my son would ask. "Not pasta again, I hope?"

I tried hard to make good nutritious meals, but it could sometimes be a challenge when I worked ten- to twelve-hour days and then came home to care for my family. I hired childcare providers to come to the house, but none of them prepared dinner. By the time I arrived, they were racing for the door.

"See you tomorrow!" they'd say, as they made a break for it, leaving me alone with tired and hungry kids. After dinner there was homework, arguments, bath time, arguments, and then bedtime storytelling. Then it was time to get ready for the next day before I fell into bed in an exhausted heap. All too soon, the alarm would wake me to put on my uniform for the next day's work challenges.

23.
SUPERHERO RANGER

Park rangers get called many different names by park visitors.

"Hey Ranger!" if they needed help.

"You asshole!" if we took away their booze or weapons.

"Help, officer!" if they needed rescuing.

"You suck!" if we arrested them.

And so on. You get the idea.

But the funniest name I was ever called happened one day at Folsom Lake when I stopped a guy and his buddy for drunk driving. The driver was so drunk he was weaving all over the roadway, and it was just a matter of time before he either seriously injured himself or killed someone. The passenger was fairly drunk, too, but he hadn't really committed any crime. He was being cooperative, so I was stuck trying to figure out what to do with him after his buddy was arrested. At this point I was feeling pretty tired, but this particular dude was in the mood for a discussion. He was young and dark-haired, a nice-enough-looking kid about eighteen years old.

"Why do you have to take my buddy to jail?" he asked me.

"I'm not. The other ranger over there is taking him in. I'm here to make sure the vehicle gets towed to safety. You are obviously in no condition to drive. Shall I call someone to come pick you up?"

"Sure. You can call my buddy Jim. Here's his number."

I keyed my mike and called Dispatch to contact Jim, which they did for me immediately.

"Okay, buddy. Your ride is on the way."

"Thanks, Lady. Hey, how come you can't just drive me home, Lady Ranger? I wouldn't mind that; you're kind of cute in an obnoxious way."

"I can't drive you because I have lots of other work to do right now. Also, I would have to handcuff you if I transported you home, and you wouldn't like that at all."

"Transport? You talk funny. Are we talking Star Trek transporting? Are you gonna beam me out?"

"I wish."

I kept thinking how much I would love to beam every young male away from Folsom Lake to a planet far, far away …

I was really beginning to dislike all young men as a species and thought perhaps they should all be sent to a desert island in the middle of the ocean until they grew up. That's *grew* up, not *threw* up, although plenty of them did the latter after drinking in the park. Drinking, posturing, shouting, vomiting, peeing in public, fighting … the list was endless. But this young man wasn't so bad. He seemed nice enough, just a little too drunk.

"Can I call you a Rangerette?" (This was in the early days of women being rangers. The public wasn't used to seeing us out there, so we were often called "Rangerettes," which was annoying.)

"Absolutely not!" I had heard this *so* many times.

"Well, what the heck do they call you lady rangers, anyway?"

"They call us rangers."

"Not lady rangers?"

"No."

"What's that thing you're wearing, underneath your shirt?"

"Huh?"

"Under your shirt there. You look all buffed out. What the heck is that chunky-looking thing?"

"Body armor."

"Whaaat? Body armor? You look like some kind of superhero!"

My patrol partner Daryl was standing next to me and when he heard this, he burst out laughing.

"Knock it off, Daryl!"

"Superhero Rangerette! Superhero Rangerette!" the young man started shouting. Now that he had an audience, he wouldn't shut up.

"Look, kid, shut up, or I will find a reason to take you to jail."

"Sorry, lady!"

"Daryl, let's go," I said wearily, as the young man's friend arrived to pick him up.

As we climbed back into the patrol vehicle, Daryl said, "You are a superhero ranger. But not in the way that bozo was implying. Think of it as a badge of courage, Rosanne. You are one tough hero!"

At this point I couldn't help but laugh. It had been a really long day, and it *was* kind of hilarious. How could I stay upset in the face of such silliness?

But listening to coworkers' comments wasn't as bad as dealing with the fallout from bad supervisor decisions.

24.
CRAZY WOMAN BLUES

There was one woman in particular whom I will never forget. One evening as the sun was setting at Folsom Lake, I got a radio call from my supervisor, Blake.

"Rosanne, could you please come meet me near the entrance to Miner's Bar? I have a young girl here who needs help."

"On my way!" I replied, imagining a young child who was lost.

When I arrived, Blake was standing with a woman who looked to be in her late thirties. She was large, with thick arms and legs, long brown hair, and a mean-faced expression. I wanted nothing to do with her.

"What's going on, Blake?" I asked, wondering what he meant by a "young girl."

"She's confused and just needs some kind words and a ride home," he told me.

"She looks like she's drunk," I said. "Why didn't you take her home, or better yet, book her into jail? Is she being disorderly?"

"No, she was just hanging around here at the entrance, and I was concerned for her safety," he said.

"Blake, I don't like this. If she's drunk, she should go to jail." The woman was staggering around and reeked of alcohol. She looked like nothing but trouble to me. Alarm bells were clanging in my head.

"Just put her in your car and take her home. She says she lives near here. I'll just put her here in your back seat."

"Blake, at least handcuff her! You don't know how she is going to behave."

"No, Rosanne, just take her home. She'll tell you her address, won't you, dear?"

To this, the extremely drunken woman nodded yes.

I didn't like this situation at all. It went against all my training, and also against all my personal instincts about officer safety. But Blake was my supervisor, and I felt compelled to do as he said, even though I saw this could be trouble. I called into Dispatch, telling them I was taking this woman to her home and that I would keep them posted.

At first, everything seemed fine. The woman, Mattie Hernandez, seemed calm and cooperative. She told me to drive to a nearby neighborhood and that she would tell me to stop when we got to her house. But as we turned onto a busy intersection, things suddenly went to hell. She started squirming around and then opened the car door while we were driving.

"What are you doing? We're still driving!" I hollered.

I pulled over to the curb to close the car door, and that was when she bailed out of the car, rolling onto the sidewalk, laughing like a fool. I couldn't just leave her there because she was my responsibility now. She was a liability to herself and others.

"Mattie, can you please get back into the car and tell me where you live so I can take you home?"

She grunted like a pig and continued to roll around on the ground. I tried to get ahold of her and pull her into the car, but she was very heavy. She was a big woman and must have weighed at least 165 pounds. The more I tried to secure her, the more she kicked and rolled. I tried to handcuff her for her own safety, but she started kicking and punching me.

I silently cursed my supervisor for putting me in this situation. Worse, I cursed myself for being in this situation when I knew better, regardless of what a supervisor said. I couldn't get a decent grip on Mattie because she was covered in some kind of oily lotion. At one point she actually rolled on top of me and ripped a wad of hair out of the back of my head. As I fought to regain control, a woman bystander came to my aid and helped pull Mattie off me. With the help of the bystander, I finally managed to get the handcuffs on. Mattie banged her head up and down on the sidewalk, and somehow, she managed to knock two of her own front teeth out in the process. I picked up the wad of hair and the broken teeth to use as evidence of our struggle later. I couldn't believe I found myself in this ridiculous scenario.

"Are you okay?" the woman asked me.

"Only my pride is injured," I told her. "Thank you very much for helping me. I feel like a dope."

"What about that woman? What are you going to do with her? That girl is out of her mind!" the woman said.

"I'm taking her to jail."

"Thank heaven, I don't want her harming someone else!" the woman replied. "Is she injured?"

"She'll be alright."

Later on, I thought about how I should have taken down the bystander's information to act as a witness. I came to regret this oversight as the case developed months later.

All during this time, my dispatcher had radioed me repeatedly to check on my welfare. When I didn't answer, she became extremely alarmed and sent another patrol unit in my direction. But I didn't hear Dispatch. I was focused solely on getting this woman to jail as quickly as possible. I got Mattie back into the car, thanked the bystander profusely, and headed straight for the Sacramento County Jail. I would book Mattie on charges of drunk and disorderly conduct and assault on a peace officer.

Then things got even worse. Mattie rolled onto her back and began kicking hard at the door and windows. I was afraid she was going to break the window glass. Thump, thump … *thump!* Her feet smashed against the window, as she started to holler. I didn't have any way to bind her feet and had to think fast.

"Mattie, calm down, I'm still taking you home. Don't you want to go home?" I asked, trying to distract her until I could get to the jail, which was twenty minutes away.

"I don't wanna go home! I wanna *party! party! party!*" she shouted, kicking even harder.

This rapidly deteriorating situation required some quick and creative thinking. I would have to convince my passenger that we were heading toward fun and frolic, while we were in fact rolling to the jail.

"Okay, I'll tell you what, Mattie. If you behave and quit kicking the car, I'll take you wherever you want to go."

"Really?"

"Yes, really. I'm a party girl, too, so we're off to a party!"

"Oh wow! You're awesome!" she cried and quit kicking for the moment. "Let's go to Vegas!"

"Okay!" I said.

"Wow, really?"

"Yes, for sure! In fact, there will be a big group of people there ready to party with us when we arrive. I'm going to call them now and let them know we are coming." This was certainly true!

She settled down in anticipation. I lead-footed the gas all the way into town. I asked Dispatch to call ahead to the jail and tell them I was bringing in a real party girl, quietly describing what had taken place. The dispatcher reassured me she had already called ahead and that an entire collection of *"partiers"* would be on hand to greet and extricate the woman from my patrol car.

I kept engaging Mattie in small talk all along the way. "Why were you drinking, and how did you get lost?" I asked her.

"I really like to drink and party. I love to cause a ruckus too. Sometimes I like to go out looking for adventure. Hey, how long until we get to Vegas?"

"It will take a little bit to get there, but not too long. What do you want to do when we get there?"

"Drink and party! Drink and party! Win some slots! Woo hoo!"

"There will be lots of guys to greet us when we get there," I promised.

"Wow, you're really cool!" she slurred. I kept hoping she would pass out, but no such luck.

Finally, we arrived at the jail. Several deputies reached into the patrol car and pulled Mattie out onto a blanket. She bucked and kicked so wildly it took four guys to control her. (Then I didn't feel so bad about not being able to subdue her by myself.) They tried to stand her up so she could walk, but she instantly threw herself onto the ground, kicking, screaming, and trying to bite the legs of every nearby officer. So, they rolled her over and carried her inside face down.

I felt compassion for her, but it had been a rough time.

"I tried to help her and take her home, but it just wasn't to be," I apologized to the jail staff.

"Please don't feel badly," a woman deputy told me. "You did your best. This is a real wildcat here."

I came back to the ranger office and booked both the wad of hair from my head and Mattie's broken teeth into evidence. I felt depleted, demoralized, and exhausted. I immediately wrote out a detailed and lengthy report, knowing this whole incident would come back to haunt me later. And I was right.

About six months later I heard from Mattie's attorney. She was trying to sue me. She demanded due process for an "unlawful arrest with injuries," and a whole internal investigation ensued. This went on for over a year as her attorney tried to press charges. It was very stressful. But in the end, I prevailed, and the case was dismissed.

There were times after this incident when park visitors needed a lift because their vehicle was broken down, or they had some other issue. I told them that I would call a taxi. It wasn't my job to transport non-offenders.

I learned a valuable lesson: stick to your training and instincts no matter who tells you otherwise.

Years later, I told the story to my kids and they both acted shocked, thinking that my actions constituted "police brutality." Then later my son became a peace officer and realized that what I'd said was true. He once gave a ride to a young couple and they behaved in an unruly manner, until he stopped and ordered them from his car under threat of arrest. From that day forward he never gave anyone a ride again, unless they were in handcuffs heading to jail. A lot of people are quick to judge a police officer, when they know nothing about the challenges we face.

While I was dealing with Mattie, I kept thinking of how angry I was with the whole situation. Never again would I allow anyone, supervisor or otherwise, to tell me how to transport someone—especially an obviously drunk and disorderly person—in my patrol vehicle. If I followed my instinct, none of this would have happened! Supervisors don't always make the best decisions.

But there was one supervisor who was a shining example of what a great leader could be.

25.
JACK ZAYNOR: THE SUBURBAN COWBOY

"C'mon, cowboy! Don't be a knucklehead!" This was one of Jack's favorite sayings.

Jack Zaynor was our beloved supervisor. Probably the greatest supervisor I've ever known. He had been around forever, and we all loved him. He was a little slip of a fellow: small, wiry, bespectacled, with a wisp of gray hair, and weighing in at about one hundred pounds.

Jack was an old cowboy. He called all the guys, "Cowboy," and all the gals, "Sissie" (sister). Cowboys and Sissies, that's who we all were to Jack. He had lived and worked on a ranch much of his life, and he approached everything, including the toughest law enforcement situations, like he was, well, a cowboy on a ranch.

He spoke in a southern drawl and started every sentence with a big, long "Ahhhh." The first time I met him he said, "Ahhhh ... I don't care which one of these idiots you wanna ride along with, Sissie, but the sooner you get on a horse (behind the wheel of a patrol car) by yourself, the better off you'll be. You don't need anyone here tellin' ya how to do your job. I'm just here to help if'n you ever need me."

I instantly loved him. I'd suffered under some pretty atrocious bosses before Jack, and I knew a great boss when I saw one. And Jack was the best one ever. He gave us encouragement, was always there for us, and rarely said a harsh word unless he was really, really riled up.

Jack's approach to law enforcement was simple: treat everyone with kindness, no matter what the situation. He would wade into the most dangerous situations with nothing more than a cup of coffee in hand. Often, he had an old corncob pipe in his mouth. Even the most hardened criminals were defenseless when it came to Jack. He'd just mosey up to a crime in progress, wave his coffee cup around at the criminal perpetrators, and scold them.

One summer day there was a big fight at Main Granite Beach with about twenty-five guys hollering and hitting each other. Jack sauntered right into the middle of the group and said, "Ahhhh, now what in the Sam Hill is goin' on around here? You knuckleheads should be ashamed of yerselves, causin' all this ruckus. Why don't you tell me what's botherin' you so much that you had to go and git yerselves all worked up like this? Lookit all the folks you've upset. Look around you, now, go on!"

The perpetrators would look into the eyes of the nearby crowd, then back to Jack, then hang their heads in shame.

"We're sorry, Jack. We didn't mean to cause trouble."

"Course you did! Course you meant it. Ain't you ashamed of yer-selves now? Doggone it, quit causin' a stir! Now lookit all the trouble you caused!" (coffee cup waving at them). "Why, when I was a kid, I didn't get into trouble with the law! I went out and rode a horse. You cowboys could be doin' the same. Quit drinkin' and cussin' and causin' a ruckus and go out there and behave yerselves!"

By this time there was a huge circle of onlookers listening to old Jack gently scolding the troublemakers.

Each one of us had a different approach to law enforcement. Go in easy, go in strong, come in with a canine unit, ride up on horseback, roll in on a bike, etc. But only Jack took the cowboy approach.

"Okay, Jack," they said. "We're really sorry."

This was from the mouths of the biggest, toughest bruisers imaginable. Fearfully big men and hardened criminals would all hang their heads in shame when Jack scolded them. In the end they would all be friends, standing around in a big circle, laughing. Many of these monster dudes came back years later with their families, looking for Jack to tell them what a difference he made in their lives. And they meant it; Jack really had a positive influence on people. We were all in awe of him.

26.
"NUTHIN' WRONG WITH THIS HORSE!"

Jack Zaynor was the ultimate Zen ranger. He was also an amazing horse-back rider. He worked many rodeos as a young man and was a trick rider, often doing stand-up riding, jumping in and out of the saddle, tapping his feet on the ground while cantering, standing on his head at full gallop, and performing other eye-popping feats.

One day my husband, Vern, was complaining that the patrol horse was troublesome. "Joker" was not obeying commands and was behaving "poorly." Jack stopped by the corral to visit and see how things were going.

"I dunno, Jack," said Vern. "Every time I try and get Joker to trot, he just ambles along. He wanders off the trail all the time, and seems to do whatever he wants, no matter what kind of commands I give him."

"Git down off'n that horse and gimme the reins," Jack scoffed. "Problem is most likely with the rider and not with the animal."

With that, Jack leaped into the saddle and took off from a standstill to a full gallop, tearing up the dirt in the corral and kicking clods high into the air. Jack and Joker careened around the enclosure so fast they looked like a blur of light. As Vern looked over his shoulder, he could see Jack coming back toward him, doing a full handstand on Joker's back, flying past like a streak of greased lightning. Then Jack backflipped down into the saddle and brought the horse to a full, four-point stop on a dime.

"Nuthin' wrong with this horse!" Jack said to the dumbfounded Vern, as he handed him back the reins and casually strolled off.

Jack was like this. His soft, gravelly voice belied the boundless wealth of cowboy wisdom he carried deep within him. He was someone to be looked up to, someone to be respected. Someone you could rely on. Someone you could talk to. Someone who would listen and dispense sage advice, if asked. He rarely ever raised his voice because people stopped to listen to what he said, and listening to Jack was always worthwhile. He was kind and caring. We always knew we could count on him. He never once lorded it over people who reported to him. Instead, he would counsel any wrongdoing in a quiet, gentle manner. I remember him telling me off one day, in his gentle way.

"Ahhhh, now look, Sissie, you might outta think twice before you go and do that again, you know? Now I'm not tryin' to tell you how to do your job, but iff'n it were me, I might try doin it another way."

"What way, Jack?"

"Well, now, far be it from me to offer advice, cuz I know yer tryin' real hard to do yer best, and you are doin a great job, ya know? But I'd maybe go after it just a little different and do it this way ..."

And then Jack proceeded to describe how he would approach the scenario differently, and why. Jack's way always made more sense once he quietly explained it. A person would have to be a fool not to listen. Sure, there were a few fools on our staff who never listened to anyone, but I tried earnestly not to be one of them. If I did something foolish, Jack would tell me, and I would make darn sure I did things right the next time. I didn't want to disappoint him. A single stern word from Jack was like getting a scolding from my father. Wrongdoers were usually called "knuckleheads." If Jack called someone an "idiot," he was hopping mad.

Small in stature but large in wisdom and courage, that was our Jack. And we loved him for it.

"You could be half right about that!" he'd say. Or "A fella might have a mind to do that, if 'n he wanted to."

A lot of the ranger staff imitated Jack and the way he talked. Whenever tensions ran high it was a great way to defuse the situation. Someone would laugh, and then speak up in a Jack voice:

"Ahhhhhh ... now look here, you knuckleheads: knock this nonsense off! Bickering comes to no good, so quit yer feudin', and get back to minding the park."

This always had the medicinal effect of making us laugh out loud and forget whatever it was we were angry about.

On his last day of work, when he retired, there was a ceremony for Jack. He was so beloved that the entire staff of all the rangers, park aids, maintenance staff, administrators, managers, and Placer County Sheriff deputies came to honor him. Reporters came to do a story on him. The music played at the ceremony was "Happy Trails" from Roy Rogers and Dale Evans. He was the kind of person who, if you were fortunate enough to meet him, you felt lucky, but if you got to know him, you felt blessed. He was the Yoda of the California State Park system.

27.
TRAINING DAZE

All state park rangers were required to do monthly martial arts and fire-arms range training. Park ranger training ... it could be like hell itself but pretty darn funny at times. I look back at the photos from those days and laugh out loud. How I survived it all amazes me.

In my early years, I looked forward to training and could hardly wait to learn all about how to defend myself and protect park visitors from harm. Initially, I also loved going to the range and learning how to shoot. I was so fascinated with how to rescue others that I even became a first responder instructor. But as the years rolled by, I began to dread the training. We all did. It was repetitive and dull, lacking in imagination, with very little practicality to it. The foundational concepts were good, but we never seemed to move much beyond the very basics. Somewhere after doing ten thousand takedowns (tackles) and twenty thousand handcuffing practice sessions, the novelty began to wear off.

"Why do we have to do this same thing every month?"

"We do it to gain muscle memory, so this practice comes naturally in real-life situations," our instructors told us. "We do it this way so that in an actual arrest you won't have to think, you'll instinctively know what to do. Also, you are required by law to have a minimum of twenty-four hours of training a year."

No "real-life situation" bore even a remote resemblance to the static training we received.

"Let's don't and say we did," I complained, as my training partners grabbed me around the neck and dragged me down to the mat for the one millionth time. Arghh! *I swear I am going to get a permanent neck injury from these endless takedown procedures,* I thought to myself.

"Why don't we do something besides attacking a passive person?" I asked. "Shouldn't we be trying to take down a combative subject? I mean, real people are not going to stand around cooperatively, waiting to be taken into custody. This is impractical."

"This is the way we are instructed to do it by our department," our trainers told us. "It's the prescribed agency procedure we follow."

"I understand, but can we please move beyond the basics for a change?" I pleaded.

The "defensive tactics" training program was based on arresting a compliant subject, and naturally, *real* people in the field resisted arrest. Most struggled, twisted, turned, tripped, bit, kicked, punched, spat, pulled, and tried desperately to get away. Some tried to kill us. Many were on alcohol or drugs and felt no pain, so "control holds" employing "leverage through pain" were useless.

When I arrested dangerous people in the field, there was often a struggle, and more than once I had to roll around in the dirt to get someone under control. Once a guy got away from me because I foolishly lightened up my grip when he complained of pain. Then it took a whole group of us to recapture him. I felt like a complete idiot for letting him get loose. He was a dangerous offender who had threatened others. I should never have lightened up my grip on him. *What a loser I am*, I thought to myself, as my buddies retrieved the offender. How embarrassing!

But even the toughest of us sometimes had to give up when the struggle became too dangerous. One of our veteran rangers told a story about how he tried to arrest a big man in a large group for being drunk and disorderly in public. But his buddies were having none of it. This was their buddy, their brother, and as far as they were concerned, that ranger was dead meat. They literally picked the officer up and slammed him onto the ground. With knives drawn, they gathered in a circle around him and were ready to slit his throat.

The ranger held his hands up in the air and shouted, "Let's just forget the whole thing! Let me go, and I'll leave you alone, I swear it!"

He was lucky. He could have just as easily been killed, and everyone would have gotten clean away. There were no other officers in the area, and the ranger had relied too long on his size and strength. He was tough, the best. But these dudes were hardened criminals, and they didn't give a damn about law and order. He was lucky they decided to let him go. All too often, officers think they have to fight hard and risk their own well-being to stop a crime, but this proves nothing. Only a fool would try and persevere in a situation like that one. Big and strong as he was, that ranger had to give up and let go of the situation. Sometimes this was the smartest choice. What price do we pay for pride?

"Why did you give up? Didn't it make you angry to let those bad guys go?" I asked him.

"Hell, no!" he answered. "Only a damned fool would insist on trying to make an arrest in a situation like that. And you'd end up dead too! Don't ever let stupid pride get in the way of your life, Rosanne. Bad guys will always be out there, but your first responsibility is to go home safe at the end of the day!"

"But what about those bad dudes? What happens if they come back and threaten someone?"

"Then we get smart and go in with a whole group of officers and take them down together! Never, ever feel like you have to risk your life and go it alone."

I remembered those words for the rest of my life.

Our agency needed more aggressive training. I understood they were trying, and that everyone was at different levels of ability. But nearby sheriff departments provided more intense training with "active" subjects who realistically "fought" with you. My husband became a deputy sheriff years later, and described how different the county sheriff training was from State Parks. He had to "fight" with very combative "subjects" and get knocked to the ground. It was painful, and training injuries were common, but these deputies were tough and prepared for the most difficult arrest situations. In the years following my retirement, the State Parks defensive tactics training program became much more like the sheriff's training, far better attuned to dealing with real life scenarios.

There was one time, however, that I was grateful for all the boring, repetitive, defensive tactics training sessions I'd received over the years. One year I went overseas to Munich, Germany on a park tourism mission. I arranged to be greeted at the airport by a young German police officer named Harry so he could show me around the area. I was hardly prepared for what happened once I arrived there.

Harry was a tall, slim, good-looking young man, with steely blue eyes and sandy brown hair. He was a defensive tactics instructor and he carried himself with a strong air of confidence. He greeted me with kindness and showed me all around his workplace, introducing me to his superior officers and colleagues and promising we would soon go to lunch. But the next thing I knew, we ended up in a martial arts training room with wall-to-wall padded mats on the floor.

"Okay, let's see what you know about self-defense training. I want to see what they teach you California rangers."

"That's okay; I don't need to get slammed around on the floor right now. I just got off a very long flight," I replied with trepidation. What was this guy expecting, anyway? I had no idea if they followed the same techniques we did. I was jet-lagged and exhausted, plus he had to be at least fifteen years younger than me, and a full head taller.

"We'll just go through a few moves and then it's off to lunch," he said with a grin. "Not worried, are you? Aren't you up to the challenge?"

Suddenly I realized that I was representing the entire California State Park Ranger workforce in that room. If I didn't go along with this exercise, it wouldn't be just a personal failure, it would also be a national disgrace.

"Okay, Harry," I said, looking him in the eye. "I'm ready!" (This was a total lie.)

For the next thirty minutes we went through a series of exercises, doing defensive moves, employing twist locks and wrist locks, throwing each other to the mat in spectacular take-downs, jumping back up, slamming down again, and rolling around to see who had the best control holds, until finally he jumped up and said:

"Okay Ranger, you pass the test! I'm impressed. You handled yourself very well."

Geez! I thought, thank heaven I didn't fail, or the whole German police force would have been laughing at me. But I realized in that moment how grateful I was for all that boring repetitive training I'd received over the years at home.

Our firearms training was every bit as static. The commands at the shooting range were: "Take five steps, aim, and fire four rounds at the target. Stop, then take ten steps and fire two rounds at the target."

"What if the target moves over there? Or there? Who is going to stand still and be shot at? In a real-life situation, they will be shooting back at us. Why aren't we taking cover? Why aren't they?" we'd ask.

"We'll get to that. In this next round, you will be firing while kneeling and lying prone to make yourself a smaller target."

"Why would I kneel or lie prone in front of someone who is shooting at me? I'd be running for cover!"

"Just do it."

Whatever, I thought. In a real shooting incident, there was no way anyone would follow this protocol. Instead, we would empty our weapon while running and taking cover, reloading, and continuously firing. We wouldn't stop shooting until the subject was disabled or dead and no longer a homicidal threat to the public. Other agencies practiced active shooting while running, jumping, ducking, taking cover, or while firing, not standing in one spot waiting to be shot at. *This is how officers get killed,* I thought.

I remember one training exercise in particular. One instructor handed us clipboards and told us to "interview" our contacts while documenting the conversation. Next, we were told to toss down the clipboards and draw our weapons when the subjects began to "argue" with us and threaten us with deadly force. Then later, we were to assume the situation had de-escalated, re-holster our weapons, and continue with the interview, then repeat, and so on.

"Begin your interview," the instructor commanded.

Then, "Draw your weapons; he has a gun and he's going to try and kill you!"

The absurdity of this exercise fried my brain. I never, ever made a law enforcement contact with a clipboard in my hand. I always kept my hands free, taking up a defensive posture, ready to go for a weapon, if needed. If someone drew a weapon on me, they were going down.

After ten minutes of this routine, I'd had enough. When I was told that the subject was threatening to shoot me, I threw down the clipboard, drew my weapon and fired at the target over and over, "killing" it dead.

"What are you doing?" the instructor hollered. "You don't shoot until I give the command!"

"Sir, you don't interview a deadly subject when they have a weapon pointed at you!"

"But that's not the way this training exercise is designed!"

"With all due respect, sir, I'm done here, and so is my clipboard," I told him.

My fellow officers gaped at me in disbelief. Then they burst out laughing. Even the instructor started laughing out loud. He knew I was right.

"Okay, point taken. No more clipboard interviews. I'll come up with something more realistic next time."

I felt bad for him. He was being a good sport, and he was a good man. And in the years that followed, the firearms training program and the tools of the trade improved a great deal. It was really tough being an instructor trying to teach a bunch of obstinate officers. I learned this the hard way when it was my turn to teach.

28.

TRADING PLACES: WHO'S IN THE HOT SEAT NOW?

Park rangers also trained as first responders (similar to a paramedic) and practiced cardiopulmonary resuscitation (CPR).

I had to instruct a roomful of fifty park staff on advanced first aid and CPR. I knew it would be no easy job teaching these war-hardened veterans. I was younger than most of them, I was still fairly new at the job, and one of only two women rangers on staff. So, why should they listen to me? The previous instructor, Saul, quit in disgust. He stopped teaching right in the middle of a lesson and walked out of class, never to return to the podium again.

I decided to preempt impending failure by pulling aside the ring-leaders before the class ever started. I'd been through many different trainings with each of them over the years, and I knew personally how cruel and merciless their pointed heckling could be. I dreaded it. It was worse than death by torture. Hell, it *was* torture. I chose the main ringleader; if I could convince him to behave, the others might follow suit.

"Rick, could you give me a minute, please? I need to talk to you before we begin class. Let's make a deal, okay? I need you, Craig, and

Donnie to cooperate with me while I'm teaching. Behave yourselves, and I'll buy you lunch afterward. Act up, and you can enjoy your boring sack lunches all week. Promise me, now, or it's no deal. You know we have to get through this stuff. If you heckle me, it will take us twice as long to get through the material. We'll be in this classroom for eighty hours instead of forty. Let's just make this as painless as possible. What do you say?"

"The hell with you! We don't have to do what you say. You're not a supervisor! You can kiss our butts!"

"No, but do you want to be here for forty hours, or eighty? One way or another, we all have to get through this training. It's either me or Tim Milo, and you know what his classes are like."

Rick gave an audible groan. Yep, we all remembered. Tim's classes were like suffering through a slow coma. Endless death by PowerPoint. His classes were a droning, draining, soul-sucking, monotonous litany, which would make anyone *want* to commit suicide on the spot. Anything was better than that. Just his jokes alone were awful.

"Okay, okay, we'll behave, but you have to buy us all lunch for the rest of the week."

"Fair enough. It's a deal. But if you act up and I have to stop the class to remind you that you're acting out of line, you're going to be sorry. I have the power to give you each a pass or fail test score, and if you fail, then it's forty more hours with Tim. Guaranteed. He's waiting in the wings. The whole damn class *all over* again ... and there will be no free lunches from him!"

"Deal," Rick reluctantly agreed. "Can we at least interrupt and tell some war stories and jokes during class?"

"No!"

"Okay, okay!"

Somehow, I survived teaching the class. Just barely. Once or twice the heckling, snickering, and side conversations started up, but I gently reminded them we had a deal.

That was all it took, and by day two they behaved like model students. Well, not exactly model students, but decent enough for park staff. Like kids in school, they had to be handled with great care. I wasted very little time talking. We spent most of the class doing practical exercises and actual first aid. Who wants to sit though boring lectures, anyway? These guys had completed first aid classes numerous times before. Any one of them could have taught the class. They just needed to be recertified.

To keep things interesting, I set up all kinds of gory-looking, gross, and disgusting first aid stations with fake wounds and tons of squirting blood. I let them take turns being the victim versus the rescuer. Sometimes "victims" burst in through the classroom doors, screaming for help with lots of drama. Whatever it took to keep them engaged, I didn't care, as long as they got through the learning. I think they actually enjoyed the arguing the most.

"That guy has a broken leg, I'm telling you!"

"No, he doesn't, you idiot. He's just drunk!"

"No way, guys, he's got a busted femur!"

"Femur? Isn't that a monkey-like animal? Why would he have a wild femur?"

"You're such a jerk! A femur is a type of ferret!"

"The hell, you say! It's a type of wolverine, very vicious!"

"Why would a wolverine be here in the park? They don't roost around here!"

"Guys, please focus on the injury," I'd gently remind them, as they collapsed into laughter at their own silliness.

"Yeah, but if this dude was attacked by a femur, shouldn't we know where it went so it doesn't attack someone else nearby?"

And so on. I knew they were all pulling my leg again, but it didn't matter so long as they got through the training exercises and passed the class.

I interspersed the training with very funny movie clips, the raunchier the better. *Monty Python and The Holy Grail* episodes were fun, but *Pinky the Cat* was the all-time favorite. This video was filmed at our very own Placer County Animal Shelter.

29.

CRITTER TALES: PINKY THE CAT

The Placer County Animal Shelter had a program on the local television station. It was called *Placer County Animal Shelter Pet of the Week*. Each episode showcased a particular animal for adoption. One day, the pet of the week never made it to adoption. The animal control officer's name was Carl, and he got torn to shreds by Pinky the cat.

The scene was shot right outside the animal shelter building, on the sidewalk next to the parking lot. It was a sunny day, and everything was going well. Carl stood confidently with the cat in his arms, looking directly into the camera. He waited for the cameraman to tell him "Go," then he began his monologue:

"This is Pinky, a domestic shorthair. He's available for adoption at Placer County Animal Shelter. He's a very loving cat."

And with that, Pinky jumped over the officer's shoulder and flew through the air on the end of his leash.

"Pinky! Pinky! Whoa, dude; I think we've got a wildcat on our hands," Carl said worriedly.

With head twisting and legs flying, Pinky leaped and bounced, clawing at the air on the end of his leash, raging and yowling. At one point, a woman stepped in with a cardboard box and tried to put the wrap on the kitty. But Pinky was having none of this. He clawed his way out from under the box, then wrapped his leash around Carl's legs several times as he worked his way up to Carl's thighs. Then Pinky went into full defense mode and dug his claws deep into Carl's groin, causing Carl to scream out in agony.

"*Yaaaaagggh!*"

Carl reached down, ripped Pinky off his thigh, and dropped him on the ground. But Pinky leaped back to the attack and gripped Carl's thigh again, eliciting another primal scream of pain from the now-beleaguered animal control officer. Finally, Carl peeled Pinky off the second time, letting go of the leash. Pinky dashed off-camera and dove under a nearby car.

"Sonofabitch!" Carl muttered under his breath, just loud enough for the cameraman to capture on tape.

"I think he went under your car, man," someone muttered.

The flying food processor won that round.

I often used this video clip in police academy training classes. It was the perfect icebreaker, causing even the toughest officers to burst out laughing. "Play it again, play it again!" they would all holler like little kids, laughing so hard there were tears in their eyes.

"If you are all good in class, I will play it again before the next break," I told them. And they all behaved like model officers.

It was the most popular video I ever showed, and I showed it for many years. Adding humor to the training is what got us through those important learning sessions. Some people wondered what became of Pinky. No need to worry about him, though. As a famous cat whose video has been viewed on YouTube millions of times, he probably acquired his own kitty mansion for the rest of his nine lives.

30.
"BANG! YOU'RE DEAD!"

There was one training exercise I will never, ever forget. I remember because I got "shot" in the back of the head.

As the actor in the back of the car "dry-fired" a gun at our heads over and over, I could feel the imaginary bullets ripping into my brain.

"Bang! Bang! Bang! You're *dead*!" he shouted at me and my partner. "Both of you, you're dead!"

There were no bullets, but there just as well may have been. For all intents and purposes, I had miserably failed the training exercise and gotten myself "killed." I was involved in an agency training exercise designed to teach us how to conduct felony car stops. It was one of those "no-win" situations where too much was happening at once.

I was the lead driver in the scenario. We pulled over a windowless, white van. I called for a backup unit, and they arrived on scene. I gave commands to the occupants inside, directing them out of the van and onto the ground. The other officers searched and handcuffed each "suspect" and put them into the back of our two sedans. Everything was going alright, when the scenario turned to shit right in front of me. What had been a carefully conducted exercise suddenly deteriorated into an uncontrollable crisis. One of the remaining passengers suddenly leaped out of the van with a shotgun in his hands. Then he dropped down in front of the van, jumping around while screaming threatening obscenities like a madman. No amount of shouting or fake shooting from me or my partners changed the scenario.

I hollered to the training instructor, "I shot that guy several times; he's dead!"

"No, you didn't," she replied. "Don't talk to me; I'm not here. Just deal with the scenario."

This sucks, I thought. They didn't want to let us control the scenario by saying we shot one of the players, even though in a real-life situation, we would have fired our weapons at this deadly threat. The reason for this was because the scenario coaches wanted us to reach a particular outcome, in this case, a no-win felony stop with unforeseen dangers.

The scenario continued while we repeatedly commanded the gunman to drop his weapon. He continued his antics while the guy in the back seat of my car kept struggling, trying to get himself loose. I told the back seat dude to keep still, and commanded my fellow officer to keep an eye on him. But there was a bigger problem in front of me with the lunatic gunman shooting off fake rounds and screaming at us.

"Drop the shotgun or we will shoot!"

"F—k you!" he hollered back, racking his weapon and firing off more fake rounds.

The guy in the backseat struggled some more. I looked over my shoulder and he stopped moving again. I should have seen what was coming next.

"Keep still!" I ordered again.

What was he up to? How long was this pointless exercise going to last, I wondered?

"Keep an eye on this guy!" I told the other officer, as I turned once again to the guy with the shotgun. That's when it happened. In that instant, both my partner and I were "shot and killed."

The guy in the back seat was a small and wiry escape artist. Turned out he had super high arches in his feet. He hid a tiny little handgun in his shoe. It looked like a toy, but it was deadly. My fellow officers had searched him, but they hadn't checked and removed his shoes. When they put him in the backseat of our car, this little guy was limber enough to slide his handcuffed wrists under his legs, reach down into his shoe, extract the tiny handgun, and shoot both me and my partner "dead" in the back of the head.

End of scenario with two murdered officers. I wondered how often officers got killed in real life because of situations like this. Afterward I realized how valuable a lesson that training exercise was. *Maybe our firearms training wasn't so bad, after all,* I thought to myself. *Maybe those instructors were right.* Those shots screamed and echoed through my brain.

I couldn't sleep at all that night. All I could think about was how my own tunnel-vision "cost" me my life. I learned to never, ever put someone into my car until I thoroughly searched them from head to toe. I would never, ever assume a partner officer had done this correctly for me. After this incident I made damn sure people were fully searched. Sometimes my patrol partners got annoyed with me for "overdoing" a search before transporting someone to jail. But I didn't care. I was determined never to get shot due to carelessness. Being a park ranger could be a very dangerous job, and we never knew what might happen.

31.

"ARE YOU OUT OF YOUR FREAKING MIND?"

Most peace officers pull over one vehicle at a time. This is the normal, accepted, logical practice. Only a fool would pull over two vehicles at once. A complete idiot would try and stop three. Somehow, on that day in Granite Bay, I used the lights and loudspeaker to stop one vehicle, and unbelievably, all eight vehicles in the area pulled over.

I was a young and fairly inexperienced officer. I had only worked at Folsom Lake for a couple of months, and before that I worked at several quiet historic parks in downtown Sacramento. At those parks I wrote some parking tickets, arrested a few drunks and vandals, and gave first aid to people who'd injured themselves. I chased errant sheep and chickens off the city streets of Sacramento and herded them back into Sutter's Fort State Historic Park, and chased illegal campers off the lawn outside the California State Indian Museum. But I was still very new as a patrol ranger in a busy suburban park where serious crimes happened daily.

The group of eight trucks were "doing doughnuts" and really tearing up the landscape. They were in an open space near the boat launch area. My intention was to pull over one truck, write the driver a citation for reckless driving, and thereby "inspire" all the others to immediately quit their destructive behavior and make a hasty departure. I never expected all of them to stop. I called in the stop to Dispatch.

"Uh, Dispatch, I have an eight-car vehicle stop just north of the launch ramp at Granite Bay. I'll be out writing citations for a while."

Suddenly, all the chatter on the radio stopped and there was a stunned silence. Then everyone started talking at once.

The dispatcher asked, "Ranger 136: Did you say *eight* vehicles? Do you need backup?"

"No, Dispatch. Everyone here is very cooperative."

I used the PA in my vehicle to instruct the drivers to step out of their car and await further instructions. Unbelievably, they all did exactly what I told them to do. They just stood there and waited patiently to get their tickets. They all knew they were destroying the park, and for some reason, no one resisted. From their perspective, here was this woman ranger in their midst who looked totally unpredictable. They weren't sure what I might do, so they just stood there, mutely, every single one.

I wonder if these guys are part of a church group? I thought to myself. *Or former Eagle Scouts?* I'd never stopped a more polite and well-behaved bunch. I considered just letting them all go, but they had already done so much damage, and their deep, rutted tire tracks were everywhere.

Suddenly, all the other rangers started talking on the radio.

"Dispatch, this is 374. I'm en route to assist 136 at Granite Bay."

"Dispatch, this is 509. En route to assist 136."

... and so on until there were a half dozen other rangers there beside me.

"Uh, thanks for coming, guys, but I'm alright. I can handle it. I didn't request backup."

"Well, we're here now, so tell us what you need. How on earth did you manage to stop all these cars at once?"

"Yeah, what the hell is going on here?"

"Nothing special," I answered. "I told everyone to pull over, and they all stopped."

"Are you crazy?"

"Nope. I'm good." I smiled.

"Guys, what say we get these citations written and help get her out of here? This makes me nervous with all these dudes just standing around," said Tom, the biggest ranger in the group.

And with that he walked over to the nearest car to contact the driver. The other rangers followed suit, each one approaching a different driver. After about twenty minutes the job was done, and all the "destroyers" had left the park.

Tom came over to talk with me again.

"Not to tell you your job, but what the hell?"

"I really only intended to stop the one Jeep, but I guess they were all together. I'm also guessing that there was some unspoken brotherhood bond between them. If one of them had to pay to play, then they all did," I said.

"Well, you're nuts, but okay. Don't be afraid to call for help when you need us. We try to cover each other's backs, you know? But we also try not to get ourselves killed. What you did just now ... well, you either have balls of steel, or you're out of your mind!"

"I strive for both," I answered.

That brought a big laugh. Tom clapped me on the back and climbed back into his vehicle. "See ya, Ranger 136!"

"Bye, Tom, and thanks!"

I was one of the guys now.

32.

THE NEAR-DEATH EXPERIENCE

I never really envisioned becoming a police officer. I just wanted to be a park ranger. But unlike the US National Parks, where you can choose to be a naturalist ranger or a peace officer, California State Parks require their rangers to be full peace officers. That is because people commit crimes when they visit parks, especially in California. Many parks are close to cities, and all kinds of crimes happen. Over the years, I dealt with every kind of crime imaginable.

So, I became an officer and accepted the responsibilities. I did my job very well, even if I didn't particularly relish the enforcement aspects. I never once shied away from my responsibilities, either. Some people would hang around the office or take on projects to stay close to "home," but I preferred to be in the field. I ate my lunch in the patrol car and stayed well clear of office politics. This kept me happy. I was really beginning to enjoy the job.

In places like Folsom Lake, we wore body armor vests (nowadays called ceramic plate carriers) all year long, day and night, winter, summer, spring, and fall no matter what the weather. We never knew what dangers might await us, and we always had to be prepared for anything. Body armor vests are designed to protect against bullets, knives, and other deadly weapons. The vests consisted of cloth pockets which held dense, removable plastic armor plating.

The strangest things seemed to happen during the off-season when the lake was low and the temperatures dropped from 105 degrees down to a nice fifty to sixty-five degrees. The skies were cloudier, the park was generally quiet, and activity was low.

"I hate wearing this armor all year, especially in winter when it feels like nothing is going on," I complained one day to some fellow rangers.

"That's when you need it the most; when it seems like all is quiet and you let your guard down." Joe Brady told me.

Hmmm, I thought. How I longed to lose the heavy, clumsy, awkward body armor, which made me look and feel like Helga the Horrible. The hardest time for this unpleasant apparel was during the summer heat, when I'd get so hot my sweat would soak into the cloth padding vest that encased the armor. The armor weighed at least ten pounds and felt very heavy and clunky, especially with all the other gear we carried.

On a typical day we would wear body armor under a military-style khaki shirt, olive-colored jeans, boots, and our peace officer protective equipment (POPE gear) around our waist. POPE gear consisted of our service weapon (generally a .40 caliber semiautomatic handgun with two fourteen-round magazines), a baton, handcuffs, pepper spray, a portable radio with cord and mike, a pocketknife, gloves, flashlight, and whatever else we could fit on our belt. Some of the guys wore a second set of hand-cuffs, but I had a small waist and could barely fit the basics.

As it turned out, my coworker's words about wearing body armor turned out to be prophetic on that cloudy, winter day. It was one of those times when I was nearly killed.

Daryl and I were patrolling Main Granite Beach when he suddenly said, "Look at that maniac over there!"

I followed Daryl's gaze and saw it: a very beat-up looking, primer-gray, four-wheel drive truck tearing up the beach below the high-water mark. The driver was slinging up big clods of dirt and racing around in circles at high speed, doing doughnuts in the mud. This was illegal; nowhere was anyone allowed to tear up the park and imperil the lives of others.

Daryl was driving our sedan, so he initiated a vehicle stop. As we approached, we saw there were two men in the truck, a driver and a passenger. The driver was a long and lanky fellow with a scraggly beard and shoulder-length, dark hair. He wore a torn-up T-shirt and dirty, gray jeans and boots. The passenger was heavyset with a filthy gray T-shirt and cutoff shorts and sandals. He wore a black ball cap turned around backward, with oily-looking brown hair sticking out in all directions. He was covered in mud.

Daryl wrote the driver a ticket. In the process of identifying him we learned that he was driving on a suspended license. We warned him that he could go to jail for this, and told him we would either tow his truck away or his passenger could drive them both out of the park immediately. The passenger was belligerent, but eventually they agreed to change places and we followed them out of the park. Daryl warned them not to return that day.

"I'm worried we haven't seen the last of those guys," I said.

Sure enough, about an hour later we saw the same truck back in the park in the same area, with the original driver behind the wheel. Except now there were two additional young men in the bed of the truck. They all appeared to be drunk, and once again they were spinning doughnuts in the mud.

Fools-times-four, I thought to myself. Why didn't they listen? Now, it was going to get unpleasant.

"Some idiots never learn!" Daryl said. "Shoot, now we have no choice but to arrest the driver, and probably the passengers too, for illegal riding in the bed of a truck."

We put the flashing lights on and pulled them over again. They had all been drinking and there was a strong smell of alcohol in the truck. Empty beer cans and whiskey bottles littered the floor. The front seat passenger, same guy as before, leaped out and hopped into the bed of the truck. He took up a defensive position near a metal toolbox there.

"Step away from the toolbox and get out of the truck bed now!" we told him, but he kept jumping around, shouting curses at us. We called for the canine officer, who came on scene rapidly as we described the situation. Ike arrived with the dog, a big German shepherd. This was good, because the situation was quickly deteriorating.

The other three men were drunk but non-combative. "Danny, get outta' that truck now!" the driver said to him. "He's my brother and he can really be an ass sometimes," he said to us.

But Danny kept reaching for the toolbox. Ike walked right up to the truck and said, "Get out of the truck right now, or I will order this dog to bite; do you understand?"

Danny finally decided to comply and got out cursing and threatening everyone.

"You're all a bunch of jerks and you deserve to die!" he screamed at Ike, causing the dog to bark and growl. Ike immediately handcuffed him and put him in his patrol car.

Daryl and Ike commenced with securing the other men for drunk and disorderly behavior, and the driver for driving on a suspended license. I stood guard, ready for anything at this point.

"Whaddya mean ... you're getting me for the same offense twice? Don't I get a grace period? You can't slam me twice in one hour for the same thing!" the driver shouted at Daryl.

"You committed the same offense twice. You were warned and escorted from the park, and you chose to come back and do the same thing. You endangered your own life and the lives of others. You are going to jail now!" Daryl told him.

"Dammit! This is unfair!"

"Shut up."

"Rosanne, why are you so nervous about that toolbox?" Ike asked me.

"Well, let's see what's inside," I said with trepidation. "I think maybe he was reaching for a weapon, and he had me real worried."

"Go ahead, we have you covered," Ike said.

I reached into the truck bed and slowly and carefully opened the tool box. Inside it, lying right on top, was a large, gleaming, loaded, sawed-off shotgun. This was an extremely deadly felony weapon.

"*Jesus!*" Daryl and Ike both shouted. "That maniac was gonna shoot us!"

"That's what I was worried about," I said. "The way he kept reaching for the toolbox made me wonder what was hidden in there. No matter what it was, I figured we couldn't be too careful."

"*Good find!*" they both exclaimed.

Danny Boy was hauled away to be booked on felony charges. The other three were taken to jail as well. Afterward, the three of us talked about what happened. We could have been blown away at close range with a sawed-off shotgun by a crazy man. It was frightening to think about.

After this incident, no matter what time of the year it was, I always went on patrol wearing full body armor. An officer never knew when someone might try to kill them, and crazy things could happen anytime.

33.

BIKE PATROL AND THE MOTORCYCLE CAMP FROM HELL

One of my all-time favorite crime-stopper contacts was born out of my desire to exit the patrol car and get out on a bike for a change. At Folsom Lake, as in many parks, a ranger had the option to patrol in a car or truck, on horseback, by boat, or in this case, on a mountain bike.

I tried to get one of the other rangers to go with me, but it was tough to pry them outside the comfort of their climate-controlled cars.

"C'mon, Bill, let's go on bike patrol; it will be fun!"

"No thanks, Rosanne; I prefer my patrol car with everything there at my fingertips."

"But we'll be outside, getting some great exercise," I said.

"Exercise is overrated," Bill countered. "I get enough exercise chasing my two little boys."

I tried again with a different colleague. "Deanna, come with me; let's go check out the bike trail. What do you think?"

"Sorry, Rosanne, but I get enough trail time on my horses," was the answer.

"But bicycling is totally different. We can fly down the trail and cruise along the lakeshore," I said, trying to get her to come with me. But it was like pulling teeth.

"Nope, I prefer the vehicle, and I like all my stuff to be within easy reach. What if you run into something or someone committing a crime? What are you going to do, hitch them up onto your handlebars?"

Hmmm, I thought. She had a point there. But I was undeterred. *I guess I'm solo,* I thought. No one likes self-propelled vehicles anymore, if they ever did. Personally, I've always loathed cars and the whole damned fossil-fuel equation. I was born in the wrong time period. I should have been a nomadic hunter-gatherer. Or a medicine woman riding my horse across the plains. Maybe I did this in former lifetimes; it felt somehow familiar to me when I thought about it. So, I got out of the wretched patrol car whenever I had the chance.

I walked over to the cobweb-covered bike shed, grabbed a patrol bike, dusted it off, checked the tires, put on my day pack, and headed down the trail. As I glided along through the oak forest, I thought *Wow! This has to be the best job in the world!* I was outdoors, unchained, and unrestrained. Why patrol a crowded beach in a stuffy sedan when I could fly down the bikeway, far away from the crush of people? This was why I became a park ranger: freedom!

The American River Bike Trail was over thirty-two miles long. It followed the American River from the city of Folsom to Discovery Park in Sacramento. It could be accessed by road from many different points along the way, including directly across from the park office. I decided to check out the stretch of trail along Lake Natoma. There was an environmental campsite along the way, and I could see how our park visitors were faring. We didn't get out on the bikeway often.

Lake Natoma is a long, linear lake in a gentle valley below Folsom Dam. The hillsides form an idyllic backdrop to the bikeway. As I sailed along, I could see the calm waters of the lake reflecting the colorful images from blue skies and the surrounding Orangevale Bluffs. Oak and madrone trees lined the path and provided a shaded canopy above. Bird life was abundant, and I could hear the trills of meadowlarks and redwing blackbirds all around me. Swainson's hawks and turkey vultures soared silently overhead. Trout and bass darted along in the clear, cool water of the lake, taunting the local fishermen to try and catch them. Deer crisscrossed the trail; so numerous I worried I might accidentally collide with one of them.

About four miles out from the park office there was an environmental campsite nestled about two hundred feet off the main trail. We occasionally checked the site to make sure all was in order. What I found there that day absolutely astounded me. There were three young men in the site. They had illegally *driven their motorcycles* up the bikeway from an access point along a busy boulevard in Sacramento. The men were in the process of destroying the campsite.

What colossal jerks! I thought. One man was hacking the wooden picnic table apart with an axe while another was tossing the pieces into a blazing campfire. This crackling fire threatened to ignite the overhead branches of a tree. The third man was lewdly urinating against a tree with his pants dropped down to his knees, in plain view of anyone who happened to walk by. Not one of them saw me enter the site.

"What on earth do you think you're doing?" I said. Still, no one noticed me.

"*Stop!*" I shouted.

They all jumped back in alarm, no doubt wondering where I materialized from. "Stop what you're doing at once!" I commanded. "Sit down and be still!" The one guy peed himself before he could get his pants back on, then he shuffled over to what was left of the picnic table to join the others.

"We was only cuttin' up some wood for the fire," the guy with the axe proffered.

"Drop the axe, now! All of you, keep your hands in the air where I can see them! You are destroying state property and that is a crime," I said in a firm voice. "Not okay! Also, this is a bicycle trail, not a motorcycle trail."

I reached for my portable radio and called for backup. This was no time to be solo with three lawless vandals. "Folsom Dispatch, I have three adult males on motorcycles in the environmental camp at Lake Natoma. I need immediate backup, please."

"Backup en route," the dispatcher quickly replied.

"How you gonna get backup when you are on a bicycle?" the lead man asked.

"You won't have long to wait, so sit tight and show me some ID right now," I told them.

They emptied out their pockets and put their drivers' licenses on the table. I called their identifying information into Dispatch. All three of them had outstanding arrest warrants. No surprise there. Anyone stupid enough to tear up a public picnic table was probably a criminal. My buddies soon arrived in a patrol vehicle, which they somehow managed to squeeze down the bike path.

"Wow!" I said when they arrived. "How did you guys drive out here? I was expecting bicycle backup."

"Not when we heard your radio traffic about arrest warrants," Bill said. "We knew we'd be carting them to jail, and that's a long way to drag a prisoner on a bike, let alone three of them! How in the world do you manage to find these things, Rosanne?"

Bill and the other rangers were incredulous. "I guess it pays to get off the beaten path sometimes," he said in amazement.

"Do you want me to transport them?" I asked.

"No, we'll handle it. You want us to drop you off at the park office? You're going to have one hell of a report to write."

"That's okay; I'll stay and wait for the tow truck to come and cart these motorcycles out of here."

A couple of months later the case came to court. The three defendants were pleading for leniency, and the judge wanted to hear my side of the story.

"Officer McHenry, how did you come to find the defendants on the day you arrested them?"

I then told my story, exactly how I wrote it in my report. The judge was incredulous.

"You mean to say that these three men *drove* their motorcycles down the trail and chopped apart a park picnic table for firewood?"

"Yes, Your Honor that is exactly what happened," I said.

The judge turned to the defendants. "And what do you three have to say about this?"

"She was disturbing us," they said. "She rode right into our campsite and started telling us what to do! She made us put down our axe and wait for her buddies to come in a car. How come those rangers get to drive on the trail and we don't?"

"Is that all you have to say?" asked the judge. "What about destruction of public property? You destroyed a picnic table to feed your campfire. You rode your motorcycles up a bicycle trail. You were lewd in public. How is this acceptable behavior?"

"Uh, we were just havin' some fun. She didn't hafta come and ruin our good time!"

"Well, here is something fun for you to think about: a $2,000 fine for each of you, plus expenses to replace the picnic table. Plus thirty days in jail for your arrest warrants. Plus all court costs for challenging this case. Now get out of my courtroom! We have no room for fools who come here and destroy public parks."

The three men turned away, their heads hanging down. They would think twice before destroying park property again. Or not. They weren't the brightest guys in the universe.

This is one story for the memory books, I thought to myself. And yet, when you think you've seen the dumbest thing imaginable, an even more clueless person comes out of hiding ...

34.

TOY GUNS ARE NO FUN

One day my partner Wayne and I received a call from Dispatch regarding a young man with an assault rifle on the Orangevale Bluffs, the housing tract directly above Lake Natoma. My partner and I raced out to the area and began searching for this individual. We couldn't find anything at first, so we split up, and that's when I saw the guy. I spotted him in the brush about twenty feet below me, creeping around, crouching low, and looking through his rifle sights at some distant object.

At this point, the most logical thing would be to draw my weapon and shout at him to drop his gun. But I wanted to warn my partner who was walking right toward this kid. So, I turned and ran back toward Wayne and told him that the kid was on the bluff just out of view. What I didn't realize is that the kid spotted me and had trotted along behind me. This resulted in him popping into plain view, causing both of us to draw our weapons.

"Drop the gun!" my partner shouted.

The kid screamed, "It's only a toy!"

"Drop it or you'll be dead!"

The kid did as he was told.

"Put your hands in the air! Do it now, and keep them there! Don't move. Keep your hands raised, or I will shoot!" Wayne hollered.

I ran over and grabbed the "gun" while my partner kept his weapon trained on the kid. I confirmed, "It's just a toy gun, Wayne."

We both relaxed a bit, relieved that the tense situation was obviously just a kid playing "soldier." He was dressed in army camouflage fatigues, and the fake rifle was a remarkable facsimile of a real gun. We holstered our guns as Wayne quickly searched the kid and found a pocket knife on him, which we kept for the moment, but no other weapons. We identified him as a local teen who lived in the neighborhood.

"Jeez, kid, are you out of your freaking mind?" Wayne said. "Are you trying to get yourself killed? What in the hell do you think you're doing out here?"

"What were you thinking?" I asked the now visibly shaken youngster. "You could've been killed, you know. Your toy gun looks real, and we could have shot you, thinking you were trying to kill someone."

"I was just pretending," he said.

"Pretending what?" Wayne demanded.

"Pretending to be a soldier," the kid said, his eyes downcast.

"You wanna be a soldier?"

"Yeah, my dad and grandad were both in the military."

"How old are you, kid?" Wayne asked.

"Sixteen."

The young man was large for his age. He looked to be eighteen, or older. But he really was just a big kid, playing war games. I suddenly felt badly for the poor guy.

"Well, thank you for wanting to serve your country, but if you want to live past age sixteen, you'd better not try this again, or you're going to get shot by accident," we told him.

"Okay. I'm really sorry. I didn't know."

"Just be careful and stay alive," I said. "Look into ROTC programs in your community if you want to go military. It's a lot safer than doing this. Or one of our officers can talk with you about the military. We have several veterans on staff."

We let the kid go. "Are you guys gonna call my mom?" he asked.

"No, kid, you're free to go. Just use your head next time. And be safe."

Too many children were getting shot because of toy guns that looked nearly identical to the real thing. All too often, police officers responded to a call of a stalker with a gun, went to investigate, and found an aggressive "intruder" with a gun pointed at them. Often it was dark. Shots were fired in self-defense, and before anyone knew what was happening, a child would be dead. This was as tragic for the involved officers as it was for the families of the stricken children. How was an officer to know the person behind the real-looking "gun" was a child with a toy? It might sound senseless, but in the split second when life and death decisions must be made, how was an officer to discern the difference? The loss of the child was an unbelievable tragedy, and the officer's life was never the same afterward.

In the years that followed, after countless incidents of children being shot at by officers chasing down "suspects" with real-looking guns, things changed. Toy manufacturers were prohibited by law from making guns that looked realistic. Instead, toy guns had to be painted in bright colors like yellow, orange, or neon green so they weren't mistaken for real weapons.

In the craziness and confusion of a split-second call, it is almost impossible to discern the exact shape or color of a deadly weapon. We just see the outline of it. There's no time to distinguish it, and hesitation could be fatal. Countless officers and civilians alike are killed every year because they are caught off guard in a real, live, shooting scenario.

What lesson do we teach our children by giving them a toy gun? We set them up at an early age to kill. In recent years, realistic-looking toy guns are again appearing on the market. Deadly weapons, real or pretend, should never be treated as toys.

35.

RAPTOR MAN

"You've got some weird survivalist nut out there shooting at birds!" a man said when he came to the Auburn ranger station on Highway 49 to report a crime in progress. He was livid.

"What's going on?" we asked him.

"I don't know what he is up to, but it isn't good! He's got a rifle with a scope on it, and he's shooting at those giant birds down there!"

He was referring to a nest of turkey vultures on a cliff along the canyon wall below our ranger station. We took the report and learned that a young man dressed in full camouflage attire was shooting at turkey vultures.

"I'll go and investigate," I said.

It turned out to be a major situation. A young man in his twenties, fully outfitted in survivalist attire with a scoped rifle in hand, was shooting at turkey vultures soaring in the updrafts from the canyon below. A raptor is a bird of prey, and although turkey vultures generally eat carrion (dead animals), they are also known to eat small animals, fish, insects, reptiles, and other prey. They are a critical part of the ecosystem. I drove right up to where the young man was standing and immediately exited my vehicle.

"Drop your weapon and put your hands in the air!" I shouted at him. He complied as I quickly searched and handcuffed him, read him his rights, and questioned him.

"What are you doing?" I asked him. "Do you know you are in a State Recreation Area and that it is illegal to shoot here?"

"I'm practicing survival routines. I plan to go on a wilderness trip soon, and I was doing target practice."

"You're not allowed to discharge weapons here," I told him. "What other weapons are you using?"

"I dunno. The usual, I suppose," he answered.

The usual? I wondered. That could mean anything.

"Okay if I take a look in your duffel bag, here?" I asked.

"Go ahead; I've done nothing wrong," he replied.

I searched his gear bag and found a frightening collection of weapons. He had dirks, daggers, switchblade knives, nunchucks, throwing stars, fléchette darts, and practically everything else described as a felony weapon in California Penal Code Section 12022. I half expected to find a rocket launcher in that bag. Having any single one of these items was considered a felony crime, much less this extensive collection. I had no choice but to continue with the arrest and transport him to jail. He was surprisingly cooperative and didn't argue with me, unlike many others I'd encountered on weapons contacts. He was clean-cut and could have passed for a soldier.

"Why do you have all these weapons?" I asked, after reading him his rights.

"A man can never be too prepared to defend against the enemy," he answered.

"What enemy?"

"Anyone who goes against me."

"Well, the district attorney will definitely be going against you," I said. "Do you realize that it is a crime to have these? Where did you get all this gear?"

"I traded for it."

Good grief, I thought. All too easy in today's world. Black market weapons were a popular commodity.

"Why were you shooting at the birds?"

"Target practice. Why not?" he answered.

Jeez, I thought. These were defenseless birds. They hadn't done anything wrong. This guy was scary. Cooperative, but scary.

I've met many hardcore survivalist types in the woods over the years. I've encountered hunting parties with illegal firearms, and confiscated all types of illegal weaponry. I've seen all sorts of strange and unusual behavior. I've even stopped bow hunters from killing each other in the woods, where they often mistook each other for wild game. One guy shot his buddy in the chest, mistaking a waving hand for a turkey head.

"I thought I was shooting at a turkey, not at a person! I just shot my friend! I've killed my friend!" the horrified guy cried.

His friend went to the hospital with serious injuries, but thankfully, he lived to tell the story.

In general, I had no problem at all with survivalists. Learning skills for wilderness survival could be a very useful tactic, and I wanted to learn more about this myself. But there were rules to be followed. All too often, people got hurt. This was the first time I caught a guy with such a wide array of illegal weapons. What struck me the most was his dead sense of calm, as though his strange behavior was the most natural thing in the world. It was eerie.

"Can't you cut me a break, Ranger Lady? I wasn't hurting anyone!"

"Well, I'm sorry, sir, but I can't just let you go," I told him. "You have a large collection of dangerous felony weapons in your possession. This goes beyond basic survival; these are illegal, deadly weapons."

"It doesn't matter," he said.

Cold, dead apathy. It made me wonder what, or *who* else, he might have shot at before I found him that day.

Yikes.

36.
BARHAWK: THE WILD MAN

The "Raptor Man" wasn't the only strange character in the canyon. One day I ran into another wild man with a whole encampment full of strangeness.

"I'm going to walk the river below Ruck-a-Chucky," I told Tim, our managing supervisor at the Auburn ranger station. "I think some of the rafting groups might be illegally camping down there."

"If you're going down there, can you search around in the area for a guy? We know he has been in there for a while, because we keep hearing about him from rafters. We've been trying to catch him for weeks."

"Why don't you just go in and confiscate his gear?"

"Well, we aren't exactly sure where his camp is. It seems to be well-hidden in the brush. You'll need to look around for it. We think it's someplace upstream and across the river from Cherokee Bar. If you find him, call us, and we'll come get him. You don't need to take him on all alone."

"Okay," I said like a fool. I was intrigued enough to do it: find a guy that had been eluding everyone. But how smart was I to do this? I wondered. *Probably pretty dumb,* I thought. Hmmm, my favorite kind of assignment.

I parked my truck way upstream where it wouldn't be seen from the canyon. Then I quietly slinked down through the brush, working my way toward the area where the encampment should be. It was very well-hidden, because it took me a long time to find it, even though I had a rough idea where to look.

The river snaked past under a gray-blue sky in the hot afternoon sun. More than once I caught my shirt and jeans on manzanita bushes, nearly ripping my uniform. It was marshy in places and my boots stuck in the muck. Wasps and mosquitos attacked from seemingly every direction in the intense summer heat. Ugh, I thought, why would anyone want to camp here?

After about twenty minutes of bushwhacking, I found him, sleeping alone in a hollowed-out thicket of willows along the river's edge. There were two long rifles shoved into the brush, right within arm's reach. I hadn't expected him to actually *be* there. He was snoring. I made a rapid dive for his guns before he woke up and tried to shoot me. At his feet was a huge bag of dried marijuana. He was obviously involved in a weed-growing operation somewhere in the area. He woke up before I could move away. I needed to act quickly.

"State Park Ranger, you're under arrest for illegal weapons and contraband!" I hollered. "Put your hands up!"

He did as he was told, but he was very squirrelly, weaving around and mumbling incoherently.

"Don't move!" I told him, as I reached for my radio to call for backup.

That's when he made a break for it. He dodged past me, jerked around to the right, then ran straight up the mountainside to the left, crashing through brush and disappearing. He flew up the hill like a gazelle.

"Damn!" I said. "Damn, damn, damn!" I'd almost had him! I should have made him lie down and then searched and handcuffed him! But I was worried about all the weapons laying around and falling into a struggle with him ... and possibly getting shot in the process. I tried to follow him through the brush up the steep hill, but I would have injured myself doing this. The brush was thick and nearly impenetrable, and the whole hillside was crammed full of poison oak. I wasn't about to hurt myself going after this fool. Anyhow, I got what I came for. I'd found his encampment. The rest we could deal with later.

As for the guy, he had nothing to lose by running because (as we later learned) he had a criminal record a mile long. He'd left behind his wallet and identifying information, several handguns, a huge twenty-pound bag of weed, two rifles, and a wide assortment of slimy-looking camp gear. He'd obviously been camped there a long time, based on the size of his weed haul. That grow operation had to be somewhere right nearby. I carried out his wallet, the weapons, and the weed. The rest I left for our park staff to come get later.

Back at the office we inventoried the gear. "Rosanne be careful out there," Tim told me. "I know you want to catch the bad guys for the good of the park, but I don't expect you to get yourself hurt or killed."

"I know, Tim. It all happened so fast. I wanted to find that camp for you."

"I understand. Just be careful in the future. You're not the Lone Ranger and it isn't worth risking your life."

Lone Ranger Rose, I thought. I liked the sound of it. This was, in many ways, a Lone Ranger job. Sure, we all backed each other up whenever we were able, but with a forty thousand-acre park to patrol, we were often all alone. I couldn't count how many times I'd been in danger. It was simply the nature of the job. I felt more like a Rogue Ranger, though.

Rogue Ranger Rose. Yep, I liked the sound of that even more.

The illegal camper's name was Barhawk. He was a young Caucasian male, about thirty years old. We never saw him again, but his scrappy-looking father came by the ranger station repeatedly during the year, demanding to get his son's gear back.

"Gimme back ma boy's thangs," he said with a toothy snarl. "Them are his thangs; you ain't got no right to 'em!"

"We'll give you his things when you bring him in here," we told him.

"He-el no! You'all will slap his ass in jail if'n he comes here!"

"Yep," we said.

"Gimme his stuff, damn you!"

"Mister, you better leave before we slap you in jail!"

Barhawk never did come for his things. Eventually we took the stuff to the dump. The weapons and the weed were turned over to the Placer County Sheriff Office for destruction. Barhawk stayed clear of the canyon after that. We searched all over for his grow operation but never found it. It was probably on someone's private property. Grow houses were all over the area, all across the state. Sometimes deputies were shot or killed when they accidentally walked into one. Green laboratories with deadly growers.

Who knows what might have happened to me if Barhawk was awake that afternoon when I stumbled into his camp? Rogue Ranger Rose might have checked out early that day. A sobering thought indeed. Fortunately, I was able to continue the work that I loved, helping park visitors.

37.
WOMAN DOWN!

People rode horses on the park trails every day. Trails went all over the park, but one of the most popular routes was the segment from Granite Bay to Rattlesnake Bar. It was about ten miles long and followed the North Fork of the American River.

The park received a call about an elderly woman named Pauline who was thrown from her horse and suffered a serious head injury. But the call was vague regarding her location. Someone hiking down the trail reported the accident.

"There's an elderly woman on the trail near Rattlesnake Bar and she's hurt. She may have a head injury or broken bones. She seemed dazed. She is lying on the ground and her horse is running loose."

People rode that trail every day, and injuries were common. But rarely did an elderly person ride all alone. We were very concerned, so several of us set out to look for her. I hiked for miles up the trail but found no sign of her. Finally, I heard on the radio that two other rangers came down from the trailhead at Rattlesnake Bar and located her. They gave the woman first aid and packaged her for transport as the ambulance arrived to take her to the local hospital.

We checked on her in the days that followed. She was in her seventies, a slim little lady with silver hair and bright blue eyes. She suffered a fractured skull and several broken ribs. She needed to be closely monitored due to her age and the risk of brain injury.

I went to see her and told her how sorry we were that she was injured. I asked her why she was riding alone.

"Why not?" she responded. "I'm used to being alone. Besides, I wasn't really alone. I had my horse with me. He's a great companion."

"Yes, but he left you when you fell."

"He was just trying to go for help."

I had to laugh at this. This old lady was spunky. She seemed undaunted by what had happened. I liked her immediately and admired her spirit.

"When will they let me out of here?" she asked. "I'm ready to go home."

"Soon," I answered.

"I want to thank all of you rangers for everything you've done. You've been so kind to me."

"I'm not the one who found you. Dana and Stu found you. I'm the dope who couldn't find you. I walked for miles up the trail, looking in all the wrong places. I'm still mad at myself for not finding you."

"Don't be. I appreciate all of your efforts. You've come here to visit me. Who wants to see an old woman in a hospital bed? It's very kind of you to come."

"That's not what I see," I told her. "I see a strong and courageous woman who survived a dangerous fall off a horse. Some people would die, or they'd be paralyzed from an accident like that."

"I was dumb enough to fall off the horse!"

"Well, I think gravity had something to do with that. Didn't you say he reared up when he thought he saw a snake? You were lucky you didn't split your skull on a rock."

"I tried to break my head, apparently. I've managed to fight gravity all my life and not get my bones busted. This time I failed. How many bones did I break, anyway?"

"A few ribs and one small skull fracture."

"Yikes! I feel like some of my brains got left back there on the trail," she laughed.

"Your brains are all still in your head," I laughed. "The doctor said you will be just fine. I think they want to keep you a few more days just to be sure."

"Fair enough. But I think my life savings will only cover the first three minutes of my stay here, so they may boot me out once they realize this fact."

"Well, that will be their loss, then," I smiled.

Pauline was a delight. She was seventy-six, and all the park staff who visited her came back with stories of her witticisms. The hospital staff loved her. She was one of those people everyone looked up to. We were very impressed with her kindness and years of acquired wisdom. She bore no ill will toward anyone, and she took the time to ask each of us about our lives. She was genuinely interested in others.

She was in marked contrast to other people I'd helped on the trail. I once helped a woman on a park trail who tripped over a cobblestone and fell. She had a broken arm but would not let me treat her. She was in her thirties with a medium build, scraggly brown hair, and a big scowl on her face. Her lower right arm was bent outward at an unnatural angle.

"Ma'am, I can see that your arm is broken. Please let me help you. I'm a first responder and I've treated many injuries. We need to secure and splint your arm, or your injury will worsen. Can I call an ambulance to take you to the hospital? You should not drive yourself."

"I don't need or want your help! I'm an emergency room nurse and I know a helluva lot more than you do. I can take care of myself!"

"Yes, ma'am, I understand. But, sometimes when people have been injured they are in a state of shock, they may not realize how injured they are. I'm very concerned for you. I need to immobilize your arm and check you for other injuries."

"Leave me alone! You can't force me to accept treatment."

I could see this was going nowhere fast. I couldn't insist on treating her, but I wasn't going to let her just walk away, either, because I had a responsibility to act.

"Ma'am, I'm not forcing you to do anything. I am just trying to help an injured person. You may not realize it or want to admit it, but you are injured. If you decide to refuse treatment, I need you to sign a Release of Liability form."

"I'm not signing anything!"

Hospital staff can make the worst patients, I thought to myself. They refused to acknowledge that a trained person in the field might have knowledge about their injured state. They only recognized the authority of another medical staff person. I could understand this to a point, but this woman was being unreasonable.

"Either you let me treat you or you sign the release form."

"I'll sign your damned form."

What a rude person, I thought. She will figure out later that she is injured, and then she'll want to blame someone else for her own lack of clarity. And that person will be me; I'm sure of it. It's just a matter of time.

I was ready for her, though.

Six months later it came. I knew it would. The injury lawsuit. I'd been through this scenario before. It was a pattern when park visitors were injured and refused treatment. After they belatedly realized that they *were,* in fact, injured, they tried to place the blame on the park staff so that they themselves would not be found responsible for their injury. This woman discovered, after her shock wore off and she drove herself home, that she had a fractured radius (lower arm bone) and that she complicated her injury by driving. Rather than accept the fact that she compromised her own well-being, she tried to sue the park staff for failing to attend to her.

"Where is the report on this?" my district manager demanded. He was all worked up and angry that we were in this situation.

"The report is right there in the district files where it has been all along," I told him.

"What? I asked for it earlier and never saw it. Her attorney is calling us!"

"Well, if you had contacted me directly, I would have given you a copy of the report right away. I don't know who you asked earlier, but I did my job and filed a full report, complete with photos of the injury site and a copy of the signed Release of Liability form. A copy should have been sent to your office as I directed."

"Okay. I thought there was no report."

"Of course there's a report. I'll make you a copy now. Please read it and let me know if you or the complainant's attorney still have questions. That woman is lying."

There were no more questions once everyone read the report. The case was dropped. My manager told me later it was a very good report. Certainly it was. I was no slouch when it came to documenting incidents. Also, I knew how to protect myself from this kind of pushback.

I never forgot this situation. All too often, park staff let these incidents go without reporting them and, months later, park visitors took advantage by filing frivolous lawsuits. Then the state is in the unpleasant situation of having to pay a settlement. Worse, employees were sued for failure to act. It could be a minefield out there sometimes, which was why it was so important to carefully document all incidents, even the seemingly minor ones.

I didn't hold my breath waiting for an apology. I was just relieved that the issue ended there. The pen had saved me from the sword.

38.
BROKEN AND BUSTED

I was on my way to check on river activity one day and there he was. The blond-haired young man lay across the roadway in a daze, his leg shattered. I parked my truck in the lane at the beginning of the curve on this narrow section of Highway 49 and ran over to him.

"What happened?" I asked him.

He just gazed at me in a stupor. Obviously, he had been racing around the turns too fast and his motorcycle slid out from under him, crashing into the guard rail and sending him flying. The impact shattered his leg. Gravity won this round.

He had a very serious compound fracture. The jagged edge of his left tibia (shinbone) was protruding through the flesh of his leg. He seemed to be on the edge of consciousness and heading into deep shock. He just stared at me, wordless, his eyes vacant. I saw many different types of injuries over the years, but this was one of the worst I'd experienced. Every day on this stretch of road I saw young men racing by on motorcycles so fast they nearly touched the ground as they roared around sharp bends in the road. Each young man seemed to think they were invincible, so they flew along the highway at breakneck speed.

I called for an ambulance. I knew they would respond quickly. I heard sirens along this roadway almost every day. This kid was so young. I guessed his age to be twenty-one or twenty-two at most. This injury was going to haunt him for the rest of his life. My professional courtesy evaporated, and I had to fight back emotion. Why was he going so fast? What is it about speed that makes humans feel they can defy the laws of physics? Why don't we think about the consequences? I sat down in the road and spoke to the young man.

"Help is on the way. You don't need to talk. Just try and stay calm. We will get you to medical care quickly." But the words rang hollow in my head.

The paramedics soon arrived, and I handed the young man off to them. I wanted to miraculously fix him, but this was way beyond my control. He was just a kid, so new to the dangers of living. But life had slowed him down.

A ranger named Rob arrived on scene and suggested I leave it to him.

"Rosanne, just go. There's nothing more you can do here. You can't fix this. I'll stay here while they finish packaging this kid up, and I'll secure the scene afterward. Unfortunately, I've dealt with incidents like this countless times."

"Rob, I want to reverse time and warn this kid to slow down, to not be shattered like this."

"You'd have to stand out here every single day of the year with a red flag. Even then, you couldn't change the way things are. Young men are reckless. It's just in their nature. They all think they are invincible."

I hate this, I thought. I wanted to do more. I wondered if there was a way to make an impact in the lives of these reckless young men. A compassionate ranger taught me how to do just that.

39.

THE GUARDIAN ANGEL

What happens on the way to the jail? When a park ranger has to arrest someone, it's because they present a danger to themselves or others. Admonishing them and leaving them in the park is not an option. They will just continue to commit crimes.

After my first one hundred or so arrests, I began to resent young men as a species. It seemed they were all crazy, coming to the park to drink and fight, drive like idiots, smash up their vehicles, and commit countless other types of unacceptable behavior. I guess my feelings must have really showed one day as I transported two young men from Folsom Lake to the Placer County Jail in north Auburn, a forty-minute drive from the center of the park. These young men were from a different part of the country, which must have had some rough-and-tumble law enforcement there. I noticed the young men were very quiet during the drive, and when we arrived at the turnoff to the jail, they were both visibly shaking.

"What's the matter?" I asked them.

"Where are we?" one of them asked.

"At the jail."

"Oh, thank God!"

"What?"

"We thought you were taking us way out into the country and that you were going to beat us or something."

Oh *no!* I thought. *These poor kids! What kind of body language was I displaying to scare them so badly?*

"Why would you think that?" I asked, incredulous.

"Where we come from, police officers are pretty rough on criminals."

"Listen, guys," I said. "No park ranger is going to harm you unless you threaten someone with great bodily harm. Then we arrest you and you'll go to jail. No roughing up."

"We're so glad. We were so afraid!"

I was shocked to hear this.

"Guys, I'm very sorry if I did anything to make you feel afraid. Please relax. No one is going to harm you."

The young men calmed down. When I got to the jail, I told the deputies to treat the kids as gently as possible and that they were cooperative and respectful.

This interaction made me rethink how to handle jail transports from then on. I talked to my husband, Vern, about this incident and he told me how he managed things. He took a totally different approach to jail transports. He used this time to counsel young men and change their lives. He would lecture them all the way to the jail, telling them about how they were messing up, and how their lives would be affected if they continued down the same path:

"You know, when I was your age, I knew better."

"Knew better than what?"

"Do you believe in guardian angels? You should. I've been sent here as your guardian angel. You are on the wrong track, buddy. This is not the life Providence intended for you. The universe has a different plan in mind for you."

"You don't look like a guardian angel. You look more like a biker!"

(This was because Ranger Vern had thick, wavy hair and a red beard. Some people thought he looked more like a biker than an officer.)

"Guardian angels come in all shapes and sizes. You need to listen to me. I learned better than to mess up my life. Someday you will want to raise a family and live like a decent human being. Do you really want to screw things up now and spend the rest of your life in jail? I have friends who destroyed their chances, just like you're doing now. They ended up in prison. You know what prison is like, don't you?"

"I'm not afraid!"

"You should be. Let me tell you what will happen to you if you end up in prison ..."

Then, Vern would describe to them, in intimate detail, exactly what would happen to them. After a few minutes, the young men would be visibly shaken. Then my husband painted a different picture. He told them about how great their lives could be if they changed their direction. He told them about the benefits of living a good life and reaping the rewards of decent living. He helped them understand how important it is to get on the right path versus the wrong one.

"So, which life do you want, the life of a career criminal in prison, or the life of a free man?"

The kids looked at him in shock. By the time they reached the jail (or juvenile hall as the case may be), the kids had bonded with Vern for life. He became a father figure to them. Many of them came back to see him, years later, with their friends and families in tow.

"Ranger, you saved my life that day you drove me to jail. I thought about everything you told me. You set me on the right path and saved me from the mess I was creating for myself. Here are my wife and children. We all want to thank you."

This happened again and again. I don't know how many young men Vern saved from becoming criminals, but there were a lot of them. Truly, he had the right idea about how to approach people, and I had a lot to learn about how a park ranger's attitude could make a huge difference. After this, I tried harder to be a 'good guy' to everyone I met.

40.
DÉJÀ VU

I hated that mean-spirited park ranger all those years ago.

We were just college kids, my future husband and I, dating and road-tripping across the Sierra Nevada foothills. We lived in the San Francisco Bay Area, so we often came to the foothills on our weekends. We'd toss a cooler, two sleeping bags, a ground tarp, and an ancient Coleman gas stove into the back of our tiny little sports car, then take off toward the hills. We camped wherever we ended up for the day. We had no money for lodging, and anyway, we enjoyed sleeping outdoors with the night sky as a blanket.

It was late one summer night when we were looking for a place to camp. It had been a long day of driving. We followed the signs to Folsom Lake, Granite Bay and arrived at the entrance gate. We drove through the gate and came face-to-face with a park ranger. He was standing outside of his patrol sedan, parked right in the middle of the road blocking traffic. His arms were crossed, and his stony glare was fixed upon us.

"The park is closed! Turn your vehicle around and depart right now!" he bellowed.

"We're just looking for a place to camp for the night." I told him. "Can we stay here?"

"No, this is strictly a day-use area. There is no campground here."

Jeez, I thought. What was this guy's problem? All we needed was a place to stop for the night.

"Where can we camp, then?"

"The campgrounds are all full!" he responded gruffly. "You need to leave this area at once. I'm closing the gates right now."

We left in dismay. I can't even remember where we went that night. But I would always remember that park ranger's terrible rudeness to us. Why had he been so awful?

Many years passed, and then I was the night ranger trying to close the gates at Granite Bay. It was 11:30 p.m. I generally used a series of statements letting people know the park was closing, starting with a fifteen-minute warning, then a ten-minute warning, then a five-minute warning, until I finally moved to close the gate.

My husband used other techniques, like putting on a fake John Wayne voice.

"Time to head outta the park now, pilgrims." Or, "This here ranch is closin' up for the night, ladies and gentlemen. Get your wagons in gear and head up to the big gates now."

Sometimes he would play exodus music on the loudspeaker to nudge people out of the park. We each tried our own methods to convince people to head home. I came to understand later that Ranger Vern's method was better.

On one particular night a young couple drove in, right past the closed entry lane and traffic cones. How could they be so dense? I wondered, irritated with the situation. I turned on my loudspeaker and blasted these miscreants with volume.

"The park is closed! Turn your vehicle around and leave at once!"

This stopped the car in its tracks. The vehicle occupants simply gaped at me in stunned silence. Obviously, they did not understand. So, once again, I pressed the button on the loudspeaker.

"This park is closed for the night! Turn your car around and leave now!"

The vehicle stood there, unmoving and immutable. Clearly, they still did not understand. I cursed inwardly as I got out of my truck to approach the car on foot. Now I was really annoyed.

"Excuse me, but what part of you does not understand that the park is closed, and you are expected to leave? Why are you still here?" I nearly shouted.

It had been a very long, hot, and busy day for me with too many things happening at once. All I wanted was to get the gates closed so I could go home sometime before 3:00 a.m. And there were a lot of gates to close in this twenty thousand-acre park. There was Rattlesnake Bar way up near Auburn, then Beal's Point, Granite Bay, Folsom Dam Road, Miner's Bar, Willow Creek, Nimbus Dam, Dike 8, Brown's Ravine, and Salmon Falls, to name a few. This meant traveling all the way around the North Fork, around the Lake Natoma area, and all the way up the South Fork. If we didn't stay on schedule with closing gates, we would literally be there all night. If we were lucky, we had two duty rangers and one supervising ranger to close all these gates. But if one of us made an arrest or if anything else came up, then we could be down to two people, or even one.

The timid, frightened voice of a woman emerged from within the dark depths of the car. It was difficult to see inside.

"We are so very sorry, madam. We were simply trying to find a ranger to ask about where we could camp. We mean no offense and want no trouble."

There were two occupants in the car: a young man, and a young woman. They were obviously from out of the country. Their strong British accents were a dead giveaway. Something about this whole scenario seemed strangely familiar to me, like deja vu.

Then all at once it struck me. Now I was the mean-spirited ranger being thoughtlessly unkind to two young people who were simply looking for a place to camp for the night.

I felt like a total jerk. I was a total jerk. *This is how jerks behave*, I thought to myself. How could I be so dense?

I apologized profusely.

"I'm terribly sorry!" I explained. "I didn't realize what you were trying to do. It's no excuse for my behavior, but I didn't understand. I thought you were challenging me, and sometimes a challenge can turn very dangerous, especially after dark ..." my voice trailed off as I saw the perplexed looks on their faces.

I told them where they could camp just a few miles down the road. I also told them the story about how, many years before, I was the target of an angry park ranger who was trying to close these very same gates under very similar circumstances.

"Now I understand why that ranger acted the way he did all those years ago, although I didn't understand it at the time," I said. "And here

I am, behaving just as badly. I feel terrible. Please accept my sincerest apologies."

They were, thankfully, very understanding. They could have just as easily filed a complaint against me for rude behavior, and they would have been well within their rights to do so. But they were very kind and grateful to learn where they could camp for the night. And we enjoyed a good laugh together about the story. They turned around and headed out, waving goodbye.

I guess it was my fate to meet with them that night. Things, it seemed, had come full circle.

41.
DRAFTED!

One day I was minding my own business, writing a report in our ranger office at Folsom Lake headquarters, and the next moment I was *drafted* to work at the Auburn State Recreation Area (SRA) as the Whitewater Rafting Program Manager, overseeing all commercial rafting activity on the North and Middle Forks of the American River.

This would eventually become an exciting but problematic job involving a new patrol raft, boat trailer, two SUVs, a staff of park aids, and innumerable headaches.

I can state clearly for the record:

I never asked for this job.

I didn't want it.

I balked at it.

I fought against it with my managers.

I was mandated to do it anyway.

I ended up cursing it, then later on … absolutely loving it.

This job began when one of my coworkers took on the responsibility to impose safety controls on the American River rafting industry. At some point he observed there were too many boats on the river. Many of the commercial rafting companies were engaged in grossly unsafe activities. They overloaded boats with too many people and not enough life jackets, put people on crowded buses with blocked emergency exits, drove these vehicles with damaged brakes down steep, winding mountain roads, had inadequate or no first aid kits, and so on. It was an endless and egregious list of dangerous offenses.

There were thousands of people in the river corridor contaminating the area with human waste, garbage, and filth. This was everywhere, on all three forks of the American River. Injuries were common, punctuated by periodic drownings. There was very limited government oversight. The South Fork was managed by the El Dorado County Sheriff's Office. The North and Middle Forks were under the management of the Auburn SRA and California State Parks.

My coworker, a ranger named Jess, initiated the program of creating and overseeing permits for the forty-five rafting companies that were tearing up the river corridor. *What a miserable job*, I thought. Why did he take this on? I figured he was trying to get promoted. Lots of rangers took on project work to gain recognition with management and move up the career ladder.

No way would I want to do a job like this, I thought. It looked miserable. Jess was stuffed into a former broom closet with stacks of permits falling all over the floor. It was a jumbled mass of paperwork. It made me want to run outside from claustrophobia. Just the thought of all that paperwork was enough to crush the spirit of any park ranger. Then one day Jess announced he was being promoted and leaving our district.

"Rosanne, I'm going to Pismo Beach as the new field supervisor!"

"Congratulations, Jess, I'm happy for you," I said with a smile. "I guess that rafting permit job helped you move up the career ladder."

"Thanks," he replied with a devilish gleam in his eyes. "I leave next month, and I want you to take over this job."

The smile dissolved from my face. I gaped at him in disbelief.

"What??? No thanks, Jess! That is a pencil-pushing administrative job and I want no part of it. You're working from a former closet in the middle of the administrative office pool. You have a pile of paperwork stacked in there and it looks chaotic. I hate being in an office. I've no interest in regulating rafting companies. It's already out of control. Anyway, I'm a field ranger, not an administrator."

"You're a great project manager. You're extremely organized and you know how to get things done. I've watched you. You're amazing."

"Flattery won't work, Jess. There is no way in hell I would want that job."

"I've already recommended you for the job to the superintendent."

"*No!* Leave me out of this. You started this program, not me!"

"They already want you to do it and will be setting up a meeting with you."

"You mean no one else will do it. I don't want the damn job. You're taking off and leaving me with a mess in your wake! I will never forgive you for this. I may come and kill you while you're sleeping."

Jess just laughed. "Just promise me you won't make a promotion out of it, or I'll never forgive *you*. I tried to promote here doing this job, and they wouldn't give me an upgrade, even though I deserved one."

"I wish they would because I don't want this job, Jess."

But my protests were in vain. The next day I was *summoned* to a meeting with the chief ranger and the district superintendent. They had already determined I was to take the job. It wasn't up to me.

How in the hell do I get into these situations? I wondered. This was the last thing I wanted, to take on a difficult permit management job for dozens of incorrigible rafting companies. They were all out there for their own profit. None of them cared about anything except making money. It would be like going to war. A futile, miserable war.

I needed to think fast. The managers had already decided I was to be the successor to this job, and I knew in my heart it was already a done deal. There was no escaping this. I remembered the saying, "No good deed goes unpunished," and now I was to be punished for being a conscientious employee. Somehow, I had to salvage the situation and rescue myself.

"Rosanne, Jess has recommended you for the Whitewater Rafting Program Manager job, and we want you to take it. You'll be the new permit manager for the forty-five different companies on the river. Jess departs in two weeks. Meet with him today to begin taking over the position," my boss told me.

"Okay," I said. "If you're going to give me this new responsibility, I have some recommendations." They would never agree to what I planned to ask for, and maybe they would get someone else to do the job, I reasoned.

"Tell them at the meeting tomorrow."

The next day I met with my boss, the chief ranger, and the superintendent.

"You were chosen to do this job," they told me. "We understand you have some ideas about it. Name your recommendations, and we'll consider them."

"This program needs to move to the field at the Auburn State Recreation Area ranger station," I said in a no-nonsense voice. "It's not effective here in this office at Folsom Lake, over an hour's drive from the nearest river access point. I need my own office at Auburn with plenty of space to work. I want a staff, two vehicles, and a patrol raft with a boat trailer so I can get out on the river and observe what's going on. I need a four-ten [four, ten-hour days] work week because I will have to work long days in the backcountry. And if I am to take on all this responsibility, I need more authority, so I will need a promotion to field supervisor status."

There, I thought. They'll never agree to all these terms, and they'll choose some other patsy for the job.

"We agree with you."

"*Whaaat?*"

"We agree. This is an important program, and we want you at the helm. We'll talk to the supervising ranger at Auburn and arrange to have the program physically transferred there. You start in two weeks, so wrap up your duties here right away."

Oh Jeez! What the hell just happened? I wondered. *They had outsmarted me and agreed to my terms. How* dare *they?* I figured they must be desperate. How could I get out of this? But there was no turning back. I made my demands, and they were met. No way out except to quit. I seriously considered this. But then it occurred to me that I could take this terrible job and turn it into something much better. I always wanted to be a backcountry ranger. The Auburn State Recreation Area was immense: over forty thousand acres of backcountry along the North and Middle Forks of the American River. Perhaps this was a way to really get way out into the field, working in more remote areas. It would also require a lot of office work, but my staff would help once I trained them.

The ranger station at the Auburn SRA was about a mile down the canyon on Highway 49, just south of Auburn. A small, single-story, wooden building, it stood on a hill, shaded by oak and pine trees. I was given a large office with lovely paned glass windows looking directly out into the forest. It was only a five-minute drive from my home. I got a brand-new whitewater raft with a boat trailer, two SUVs, and a staff of two park aids: Jennie and Mason. Jennie liked doing the office work, and Mason enjoyed setting up the raft and boating gear. However, I made sure they both knew how to do the *whole* job, so they were interchangeable. They were excellent staff and I adored them. A year later we were joined by a third park aid named Sandy.

AUBURN STATE RECREATION AREA RANGER STATION

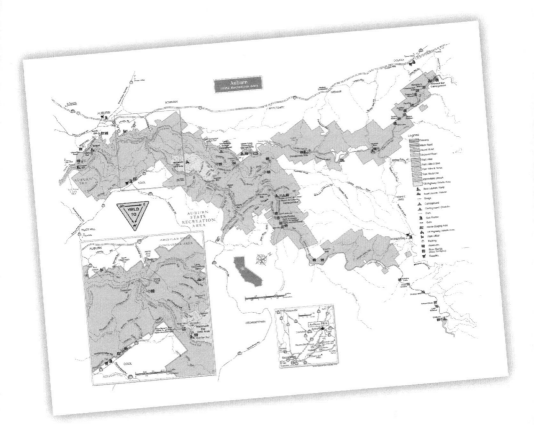

MAP OF THE AUBURN STATE RECREATION AREA

I started work on New Year's Day in 1988. I spent the winter working in the office setting up the new permit system and reaching out to the rafting company managers and staff. This felt like stepping directly into open warfare, because most of them did not welcome State Parks interference in their business operations.

During the first few meetings, I felt like I was in an intense war zone dodging shrapnel.

"We don't want State Parks telling us what to do! We've been running the river long before you guys created this so-called recreation area, and we have the first rights to the river corridor!"

"Yeah! You guys have no place telling us how many rafts we can run on the water! You don't know anything about whitewater! Get out of our way and leave us alone!"

"Excuse me, everyone," I said. "The American River corridor is largely within State Parks oversight, and it belongs to the public, not the rafting companies. My duty is to make sure you run a safe river rafting operation. At present, the situation on the river is out of control. There are too many rafts all trying to launch at once, and there are major congestion points along the river where boats bunch up and create issues. Your boats don't have adequate safety or sanitation equipment. Many of your staff are driving unsafe vehicles in need of repair. I'm here to work together with you on this, but things need to change."

"The hell you are! You guys step in here and try to tell us ..."

"Everyone *shut up right now!*"

It was Jake Wrangler, one of the biggest rafting operators on the river. He stood up and walked to the front of the room to stand beside me.

"Every last one of you, sit down, shut up, and listen! If you want to continue operating on the river, we will have to work with State Parks. Otherwise, your permits will be pulled. Now listen up and work with Rosanne, or we will end this meeting right now. If this meeting ends without resolution, there will be no permits this season. Without your permits you will be terminated from all river activity. Is this clear?"

Wow, I thought. *This guy was really in charge.* A couple of other big company leaders also stood up and openly sided with Jake. Apparently, the larger companies were sick and tired of all the chaos with too many boats on the river at once. They wanted law and order so they could operate effectively. If I could work with the industry "bosses," I might be able to bring some order to the chaos. But I could see this job wouldn't be easy. In fact, it would be a huge uphill struggle. I seriously thought again about quitting.

I thanked them for their help, regained control of the meeting, and somehow lived through the rest of it. Then I went home and collapsed. I was exhausted, and I felt like screaming. *This job sucks*, I thought. *No wonder Jess wanted to promote out of there, and no wonder no one else wanted this awful responsibility.*

I led several more meetings that winter. By springtime, the new permit system was in place. My new park aids were ready for the field. I was slowly starting to feel hopeful.

"Okay, guys, let's get out there and see where we'll be working," I said to Mason and Jennie.

We set out on the backroads. They were in dreadful shape. We crashed and bumped along, dodging boulders and potholes, trying not to drive off cliffs on the steep mountain roadways. The canyons were beautiful. Deep, steep, and spectacular, with emerald green, clear-running waters at the bottom. We mapped out all the boating put-ins and take-outs, along with the nearby camping areas and access points to each.

Our job would be to have a presence on the river and observe how well the rafting companies were following the rules. We would check for life jackets, safety gear, helmets, first aid, sanitation, transport vehicle safety, and a long list of other things. The rafting journey was nine-and-a-half river miles from Iowa Hill Bridge to Ponderosa Bridge on the North Fork, and fifteen river miles from Oxbow to Greenwood on the Middle Fork. Some companies went all the way to the Confluence at the Highway 49 Bridge, but most ended their journey at Greenwood.

MIDDLE FORK AMERICAN RIVER, WITH THE AUTHOR IN THE MIDDLE. PHOTO COURTESY OF MIKE LYNCH, AUBURN SRA.

"We really need to be on top of this, guys," I told them.

"You'll need to drive out to each access point twice a week and observe. Report everything to me. I need to know what is happening out there. I'll be on-site too, as often as I can."

We had a new raft with all the gear, the best we could buy. We had two trucks, and a boat trailer to carry the raft to the launch and take-out points.

"When do we get to go out in the raft?" Mason asked. He couldn't wait for this.

"Soon," I told them, "Very soon. But be careful what you wish for, because the river is full of surprises."

I formed a Whitewater Advisory Committee from local citizens who had river boating and resource conservation experience. We solicited their input on the rafting corridor management. We needed to have public support for our operation, because we were under close scrutiny with our new operation. I created a database of information on the entire operation, something we could all use to enter data.

Finally, in May we were ready to get our raft onto the river. We waited for the river flow to rise enough so we could get over all the obstacles, but we also needed to be careful not to go out when the water was running too fast. That was when accidents could happen.

We were soon underway, and photos were taken of our maiden voyage. None of us had piloted a raft before, so we hired a rafting guide. It would be just a matter of time until we could do it for ourselves. Mason was keen to learn and so was I, so we watched all the other guides carefully to help us pick up these critical skills. We planned to attend whitewater rafting guide classes. There were certain points along the river that were extremely dangerous: Tunnel Shoot, Ruck-a-Chucky, and Murderer's Bar on the Middle Fork, and Chamberlin Falls on the North Fork were places where accidents often happened. Sometimes these were fatal.

**OUR MAIDEN VOYAGE ON THE MIDDLE FORK, AMERICAN RIVER.
PARK AID JASON SOMARA ON FRONT LEFT,
COMMERCIAL RIVER GUIDE IN CENTER,
AND THE AUTHOR ON FRONT RIGHT.
PHOTO COURTESY OF AUBURN SRA.**

RANGER JORDAN FISHER SMITH AND THE AUTHOR OUTSIDE
THE AUBURN STATE RECREATION AREA RANGER STATION, 1988.
PHOTO COURTESY OF JORDAN FISHER SMITH, THE *NEW YORK TIMES*
BESTSELLING AUTHOR OF *NATURE NOIR* AND *ENGINEERING EDEN*.
FOR MORE ABOUT JORDAN PLEASE VISIT:
HTTPS://JORDANFISHERSMITH.COM/

ASRA Rangers 1988

**AUBURN STATE RECREATION AREA RANGERS, 1988. TOP LEFT TO RIGHT:
JOHN CLEARY, GREG WELLS, ROSANNE MCHENRY (AUTHOR), STEVE
LUMLEY (CALIFORNIA DEPARTMENT OF FORESTRY AND FIRE).
BOTTOM LEFT TO RIGHT: MIKE VAN HOOK,
MIKE LYNCH, AND JORDAN FISHER SMITH.**

THE AUTHOR IN DRESS UNIFORM WITH MICHAEL G. LYNCH, CA STATE PARK RANGER, HISTORIAN, AND RETIRED PARK SUPERINTENDENT OF THE AUBURN STATE RECREATION AREA. LYNCH IS ALSO THE AUTHOR OF SEVERAL BOOKS, INCLUDING *RANGERS OF CALIFORNIA STATE PARKS: OVER 125 YEARS OF PROTECTION AND SERVICE.*

42.
MURDERER'S BAR RAPID

It was a hot, hot, hot July day. We received a report about a fatality at Murderer's Bar on the Middle Fork. A group of amateurs from Silicon Valley had rented what we called a "rubber ducky" raft, one of those cheap plastic inflatable boats you can buy in any drugstore. They should print these words in bold letters on the boxes: **Do Not Use These on Moving Water or You Could *Die!*** It was like giving a toy pedal car to a little kid and putting them out on the freeway.

This group of five technology workers, who knew nothing about rafting, had arrived at one of the most dangerous rapids on the Middle Fork American River. Murderer's Bar got its name from the California gold rush period when a group of miners got into a gun fight in the 1850s, and several people were shot. It was a dangerous, rocky, S-turn rapid where even the most experienced rafting companies would often "high side" (lift up dangerously to one side) and lose people from their boats. Serious injuries there were common, and on that day, it claimed a victim. Mason and I responded to the scene to take the report.

When we arrived at the river, we immediately found the group surrounded by countless other boaters. It seemed strange to see four grown men crying, but they were understandably distraught. They were all young men, very new to California, and the man who died was named Teddy.

"We got caught in the current, you see," they said. "The waters carried us along too fast and the boat suddenly turned over on the rocks. We had no idea this could happen. Teddy! Oh Teddy!" And they all started crying again. Teddy was lying awkwardly in an eddy at the bottom of the rapid. An overwhelming sadness hung in the air; I could feel it emanating off all four of these young men who had unexpectedly lost a dear friend within the space of seconds.

Mason was heartsick and so was I. As a young man, Mason was unsure how to behave so he chose sick humor. "Hey, there's Teddy in the eddy!" he said with an uncomfortable laugh.

"Mason, I understand how you feel. This is awful, and I know you are desperately trying to cover up the fact that you feel very sad. I can see it in your eyes. But please don't try to make light of it. These young men are devastated. Please go help them lift Teddy out of the water and cover him from view."

Mason did as I asked. We both did what we could to comfort the others.

"We're so sorry for all of you," I told them. "We will get you transported out of the canyon to a safe location. We will also make sure Teddy is transported to the coroner's office. Please let us check you for injuries and make sure you are alright," I said.

I also calmly explained that the craft they chose was deadly on a river like this, and never to try anything like this again. They nodded in solemn agreement. Several sheriff deputies soon arrived. They drove in on the gravel road just downriver, like we did.

"We'll take it from here. We can transport these other party members back to their vehicle, and get the body to the coroner," one of them said.

"Thanks so much, guys," I said. "Can you please give me the report number so we can coordinate later?" I asked.

"Sure thing," the deputy told me.

"Thanks again, all of you," I said. I was truly grateful for their presence there.

I knew things like this happened all the time, which was exactly why we were here on the river, to help educate the public about the dangers of whitewater rafting and to regulate the industry, so that unsuspecting people like Teddy didn't have to die. But we couldn't control the sales of "rubber ducky" boats like this one—fake boats that claimed lives. I felt heartsick for this young man, his friends, and his family.

Several people drowned every year on the river. Not just in rafting accidents, but also while swimming and wading in the rapid waters at the base of bridges. Teenagers jumped from bridges and suffered broken bones or fractured skulls. People wading into rapids got caught in "strainers" or submerged objects like trees, which could trap unsuspecting swimmers in the current and pull them under. No one was immune to the dangers, and far too many people believed they were infallible. The river was indifferent. It was beautiful, deep, dangerous, compelling, and unforgiving. It could carry you along in a raft, or pull you underneath in a heartbeat, dragging you down into its cold, dark depths. The river was deadly, and it didn't care.

43.

TUNNEL CHUTE
SPECTACLE

On the upper Middle Fork of the American River is a dangerous rapid called the Tunnel Chute. In the 1860s, during the California gold rush, a mining group diverted the river away from its channel at a horseshoe bend. They did this by blasting through solid rock, creating a steep channel. Then they mined the river gravel left behind in the horseshoe bend, looking for the placer gold that was deposited in the ancient river sediments.

The upper part of the rapid was called "The Chute." This was an eighty-foot-long, straight section where the river water shot rapidly through a treacherous, bumpy, narrow slot. Below The Chute, the water pooled at the base, then carried rafters through a ninety-foot-long man-made cavern called "The Tunnel." Hence the name "Tunnel Chute."

This roller coaster ride through rapidly churning water, followed by a big, dark, echoing tunnel, was an extremely popular attraction to river rafters. They came from all over the country to go on this thrill ride.

Unfortunately, this dangerous rapid caused major injuries as people popped out of rafts in The Chute and banged up their bodies against the solid, jagged rock. Broken bones and skull fractures were common.

Fatalities happened every year. Yet countless people kept on coming for the thrill of the ride.

I didn't want to take our raft through The Chute. There was a way to portage (carry rafts and gear) around the rapid by clambering along the trail on river left, but it took a lot of effort to do this. Passengers and gear had to be removed from the boat and portaged along the trail. The empty raft could then be sent through The Chute using ropes and retrieved at the base of the rapid. Most of the rafting companies chose to run the Tunnel Chute with people and gear in the rafts, because this was the easy and exciting way through, assuming no one in the party washed out of the boat and became injured. As Whitewater Rafting Program Manager, I felt it was our duty to set an example and portage around the rapid. So, this is what we did, every time.

"Hey, Rangers!" Everyone would shout as they passed us up on The Chute.

"Whatsa matter? You too scared to run The Chute? Sissy rangers!" they'd cry as they sailed on by.

"Keep your life jackets and helmets on!" I'd holler back.

I didn't care if they thought we were cowards. I had witnessed the kinds of injuries whitewater rapids caused. I'd been through the Tunnel Chute in a boat with rafting groups before I took on this job. I didn't enjoy the ride and thought it was an unnecessary risk to life and limb. Too many life-flight helicopters had rescued injured people here over the years. I didn't want to join the ranks among the injured or dead.

One day, our California State Parks Director announced that he was coming on patrol with us. *Uh-oh*, I thought. Just what I needed, a high-ranking officer in the boat, trying to tell us what to do.

"I'd really prefer not to have the Director on a rafting ride-along," I pleaded with my manager. "We're still trying to establish a presence on the river, and this is not the best timing. Please reschedule," I said. "We're not ready for this yet, maybe later."

"I'm afraid we have very little to say about it. He's our top boss. You can opt out of going if you want," my manager told me.

"What? And leave our patrol raft in the hands of bureaucrats? I don't think so!"

My attitude was justifiable. State Parks directors were political appointees. Generally, they knew very little about field operations and even less about how to run a state park operation. There were some exceptions, and some very good directors. But then there were some who knew nothing about parks management. This director had never even worked as a ranger.

I dreaded this day. We launched that morning and everything went alright. I explained the route, what we would see and do, and what to expect. Then we arrived at the Tunnel Chute. I explained why we didn't run The Chute and how dangerous it was. I held my breath because I could see what was coming next. Commercial rafting boats were already careening through The Chute, their occupants hollering with glee as they crashed and bumped through the tumultuous rapid. As expected, several occupants washed out of their rafts and had to be fished out of the water. But this only added to their overall excitement. The threat of danger seems to dazzle humans, the more perilous the better.

People can be such idiots, I mused to myself. *Didn't they understand the danger?*

One of the director's entourage swaggered up to my side. "The Director wants to make the rafting run through the Tunnel Chute," he informed told me. It sounded more like a command than a request.

"Not a good idea," I countered.

"Nevertheless, I think we need to accommodate his wishes."

"If we do that, we are going to look like hypocrites," I said. "We constantly advise these commercial operations not to run the Tunnel Chute. I'm not comfortable changing our stance here in front of everybody, and violating our own safety policy. People get hurt here every day. I've seen the injuries and the fatalities. I can give you the statistics. We need to show public leadership."

"Well, if the Director says it's okay, then this is what we'll do."

This made me angry. I could clearly see that I was outranked and outnumbered. But just because this man was the Director, it didn't give him the right to force our hand like this. He should have respected the "safety-first" image we were trying to convey. He wasn't the one who had to respond to rescues when people were injured.

All the rafting groups on the river had stopped to watch us and see if we were going to violate our own principles. It felt like we were in the center of an arena. Because we were. All eyes were on *us* now.

"Go on, Rangers! Is Smokey scared? Cowards! Liars! You guys suck!" and so on, as more and more boats pulled up to watch the developing spectacle. Even my own staff members were beginning to cave, fearing retribution from the high-level bureaucrats in our boat if we dared to challenge the Director's authority. This infuriated me, but I could see it was pointless to resist.

"Okay," I said. "If you insist on doing this; if you are going to force the issue, then go ahead. Take the boat through the Tunnel Chute. Shout and laugh and get your picture taken. (A commercial river photographer was set up on a rock above The Chute to take for-profit photos). But I'm not going with you. As Whitewater Rafting Program Manager, I have an example to set here, and I'm not about to compromise on this. I'll walk down and meet you at the base of the tunnel, and for the record, I want you to know that I completely object to this."

The men all looked at each other. The entire scene was suddenly silent, with everyone waiting to see what would happen next. The Director's group conferred. His spokesman said, "Okay, we do it your way, but the Director is very disappointed."

"At least he'll get back to his office without injuries," I answered.

In the years that followed, more and more guides learned how to navigate the Tunnel Chute without injuring their occupants. This involved making everyone hunker down inside the rafts with their paddles in the air. We were happy to see this. And much later, after I promoted and moved on, some of my successors learned to run the patrol raft through the Tunnel Chute without injury. But I still thought it was a dangerous risk, and I never regretted standing my ground on that day. It was my job to convey a good public image for everyone's sake. Sometimes that means you make an unpopular decision. It wasn't about control; it was all about common sense.

"You should have done what the Director said," my supervisor told me later.

"So, fire me. I made what I believed was the right choice, with over a dozen rafting companies watching our every move. If we ran that rapid, we would have lost face with them all. Try enforcing the rafting permit regulations then!"

"All the same, you should have conceded."

"I did! I told them to run through the rapid without me in the boat!"

"You said that?"

"Of course! Look, you put me in charge of this program. Either back me up, or find someone else to take on this responsibility. I don't see anyone else waiting in the wings to do this job, and I really don't need the stress."

Then I went home, angry with being challenged for doing the right thing. They could all take a flying leap straight into the river for all I cared.

Nothing more was ever said about it, and the following year I was given a department-level safety award for job excellence.

44.
LAST CHANCE OUTHOUSE

Just upriver from the Tunnel Chute at Last Chance Rapid was a miner's camp. People had camped in the area since the gold rush, and the locals did a good job of keeping the area clean.

But with more and more rafting groups inundating the area, sanitation was becoming a huge problem. The rafting companies fed their guests breakfast at camp, then drove them for over an hour to the launch point. By the time the rafters got to the first scheduled rafting stop at Last Chance Rapid, people were desperate for a "restroom break."

Except there were no restrooms there. Imagine a scene with forty-five different rafting companies, each with up to seven boats per company, and each boat filled with eight people, all emptying out at the same location. It was a literal shit show and it had become a public health hazard. We were concerned about a disease outbreak, and the local miners were understandably livid.

"These damn rafting companies come through here and let their people shit all over the place. They drop used toilet paper everywhere and leave their disgusting filth behind!"

"They are supposed to carry portable toilets for their passengers," I told them.

"Oh really? You tell that to several hundred people all coming through here at once! Do you really think these bozos are gonna poop in a can? Get real, Ranger Lady!"

Uh-oh, I thought. *This is a serious problem.* I again thought about quitting my job. *Why am I doing this?* I was beginning to hate everyone on the river. I wished a giant wave of water would sweep through and flush every last person and all their gear out of the canyon.

But I realized that the miners were right. This situation was out of control. It was an abomination. I could see crusted feces all over the rocks, and everywhere, toilet paper fluttered about in the breeze. Ugh, what a mess!

The river rafting corridor wound through United States Forest Service (USFS), Bureau of Reclamation, and California SRA lands. We all had to work together to manage it. The obvious solution at this location was to install pit toilets and assign someone the responsibility of managing them.

This meant I was literally in the shithouse business, and this was the last thing I wanted to deal with. I met with the rafting company bosses, US Forest Service District Ranger Marlin Berger, and our manager to discuss how to resolve the problem. We also discussed the problem with the advisory committee to elicit ideas. Where would the money come from to build the toilets? Who would build them? And equally important, who would service them? The only road down to the site was a bumpy track from a remote location outside of Volcanoville, northeast of Georgetown. It was in the middle of nowhere.

"Okay, guys, how are we going to deal with this?" I asked at an interagency roundtable meeting.

"I'll work to get these installed," Marlin said. "We will need two deep vault toilets permanently secured on the site, set back at least one hundred feet from the river. But the rafting companies will have to service them and keep them clean. Our staff doesn't have the resources to do this. The rafters are the primary ones who will be using the toilets. It should become their responsibility."

This seemed logical enough. I met with the rafting company leaders and got agreement from them. They wanted a solution as much as anyone.

"We need to get this done soon, Marlin. What's our timeline?" I asked.

Marlin was a tall, lean, soft-spoken, no-nonsense type of guy. He was pragmatic and easygoing, and he knew how to get things done. He sized me up, looked me in the eye and said, "A year, but we need it now, so it could be done within four to six months if you help me organize it."

"I can't go out there and build it, Marlin. I don't have the skills or the time to devote to it."

"I'm not asking you to help build it. I'm just asking for your help organizing the project."

"Sounds fair to me. I'll help handle all the contract paperwork and the administrative details if you can manage the on-site construction."

"Deal," Marlin said.

We met a number of times over the next several months. We decided to charge an annual fee to every rafting company on the river to cover the cost of building and maintaining the toilets. It took a lot of effort to accomplish this, and it fell to Marlin and myself to organize and implement the construction. I learned a lot about vault toilet construction that season, more than I ever wanted to know. Marlin was the real hero, though, ensuring that all the plans turned into reality.

Ah, the life of a ranger! Installing pit toilets in the backcountry was not what I had signed up for when I chose my profession. But eventually the day came when we were able to celebrate the achievement. The toilets were done! Looking back, I wish we'd staged some sort of formal celebration, something funny. We should have brought in an "Outhouse Blues Band," or something. I remember going to the site one morning and talking with the local mining and rafting population. The two groups still hated each other, but at least now the site was clean, and they were no longer at war. The rafting companies had worked with crews to clean up the mess in the area.

"Thanks for cleaning up their act!" one of the miners told me. "To be honest, we appreciate the shithouse too, and we'll help keep it neat."

The locals weren't known for genteel language. They pretty much said what they said, and to hell with what the rest of the world thought. Then, the quiet peace of the morning was shattered. "Those miners are using our toilets!" one of the rafters complained.

"Shut up, jackass! These toilets belong to all of us, not just you rafting jerks!" one of the miners shouted back.

Uh-oh, I thought. The celebration was over. Time to depart.

"You're welcome," I told them. "Enjoy the new installment in good health!"

45.

DOWN AND OUT
AT RUCK-A-CHUCKY

I had a great job. A really great job. But there were some days I thought it might be better to beg for coins in the street. Being a public servant was very challenging at times.

The rafting run along the Middle Fork of the American River from Oxbow Dam to the Greenwood takeout was about fifteen miles. Greenwood takeout is just below the Ruck-a-Chucky rapids. The Ruck-a-Chucky falls were so named for the clattering noise of rocks rumbling through this formidable notch in the canyon. The name also may have come from the gold mining days when the camp had a reputation for terrible food: "rotten chuck" may have evolved into "ruck-a-chucky". Either way, the name was unique!

Most rafters considered Ruck-a-Chucky to be a class six, "un-runnable" rapid. The majority of groups portaged around this extremely dangerous, S-turn rapid, but every year there were some who ran it, and injuries often resulted. The steep, vertical canyon walls rose one hundred feet straight upward in a narrow slot. Towering boulders stood guard over water cascading downward in a thundering crescendo.

Most of the companies took out their boats on the right side of the river, just below the site of the old Greenwood crossing. There was once a bridge there, but it had washed out years before in a flood. That point along the river was a logical choice for takeout. A long, bumpy, but serviceable gravel road led down there from the Auburn Foresthill Road above. The boating takeout spot is a day-use area with a parking lot and river access. Immediately upriver is the campground, a series of a dozen scenic sites along the river.

The problem was the steep hillside leading from the parking lot to the river. There was no easy way to drag people, boats, and gear up the hill to the waiting vehicles. It was bad enough on dry days, but when the river was running high from late-season rain or from a water release coming out of the Oxbow Dam upriver, the hillside became a dangerous slip and slide. Some boaters tried to take out in the campsites upstream where the ground was more level, but this led to open warfare between campers and rafters, and things could easily turn ugly.

"This is our campsite, you rafting assholes!"

"Shut up, you jerk campers! You don't own the river!"

And so on. Their language was often far worse.

It was clear that something needed to be done to help people get on and off the river quickly. Some rafters, particularly the amateurs in little rubber ducky rafts, liked to launch from here, then take out at Mammoth Bar, about seven river miles downstream. Between rafts and kayaks putting in and others taking out, there were big piles of gear everywhere, and too many people clambering around at once. Things could get very heated and fights often broke out.

"Get your damn truck outta my spot! We were here first!"

"Get lost, or I'll slash your damn tires!"

"Try that and I'll shoot you, you bastard!"

And so on.

"What is the solution to this problem?" I asked my manager.

"Around 1:00 or 2:00 p.m., all the rafting groups want to take out at the same time. Plus, all the amateurs are trying to launch. Sometimes there are fifty to one hundred people or more there all at once with paddles flying, boats getting dragged up and down the slope, gear trucks backing up and down, and people nearly getting run over. It's total bedlam!"

This situation was mirrored on the North and South Forks of the American River as well. Each commercial rafting company was assigned a specific launch time so that everyone wouldn't arrive at takeout at once. But all it took was for two or three groups to be there together before fights broke out. If alcohol was involved, then fists would start flying.

"We've already drafted preliminary plans for a takeout stairway to be built at Greenwood," my manager told me. "We just need to get it done. Let's set up some meeting times with the CCC [California Conservation Corps] crew leaders to get this project underway. I can help you with the meeting coordination, and then you can move things along."

"Thanks, Tim. I'll get right on this."

Wow, I thought. *This job keeps growing more complicated.* I already had too much to do, but this was an obvious necessity. Each year there were more and more people on the river. We needed to do a better job managing it, somehow.

We met with the CCC crews several times that spring to finish drafting plans for a sizable stone staircase to be built at Greenwood takeout.

It was about thirty feet wide and fifteen steps tall; large enough to allow multiple groups plenty of space to carry equipment and boats back and forth from the road to the river. We also widened and graded the parking area above to accommodate all the vehicles. It was common to see thirty or more trucks and cars there at once, in a parking lot originally designed for ten vehicles.

Fortunately, there were lots of CCC crews in the area. Many of the crew members were young adults looking for job training, and the CCC provided a helpful venue for them to learn good construction skills. Crew leaders worked with State Parks staff to complete projects like this all over California. The steps were constructed from locally quarried limestone and serpentine rock. These were then fitted together and cemented into place. The finished stairway was a work of art. We used a program of education and signage to direct rafters to use the steps.

"Hey, Rangers, good job on the steps! You gonna put in some more steps at Oxbow? How about Ponderosa? Salmon Falls?" (And so on, as they named congestion points on all three forks of the American River.)

State Parks managed the North and Middle Forks of the American River because these were part of the Auburn SRA. The South Fork was largely managed by the El Dorado County Sheriff. A section of the South Fork ran right through Marshall Gold Discovery State Historic Park, and there were big battles going on there, too, between rafters and picnickers.

"One thing at a time," we told them.

I had a big job with many different challenges to it. Another one involved mapping landing zones for helicopters.

46.

FLYING HIGH

Rafting injuries on the river happened often, and nearly always in remote stretches of the canyon that were inaccessible by roads. Weekend warriors from office environments often came here seeking outdoor thrills. They flew in from all over the West to join up with commercial river outfitters and raft down the American River. The most serious injuries happened along the roughest and most remote sections of the canyon, hours away from medical help. Often, a helicopter had to fly in to airlift people suffering from severe head injuries, compound fractures, heart attacks, and other serious conditions. Minutes could count getting injured people to critical medical care in time, and a life-flight helicopter was often the only way to save lives.

California State Parks often teamed up with the larger sheriff agencies and with the California Highway Patrol (CHP) for airlift rescue. But, for river rescues to work effectively in places where radio coverage was scarce or nonexistent, the air crews needed to know where the landing zones lay along different points on the river.

As the Whitewater Rafting Program Manager, it was my job to fly the canyon each season with the flight crews and map out these zones, then mark the spots using GPS. Sometimes a landing zone was as small as a sand bar, and these changed with the seasons.

I met with the helicopter crew at the California Forestry and Fire Department (Cal Fire) helipad, just a short distance from our ranger office in nearby Bowman. They picked me up, handed me a helmet with earbuds and microphone, and away we flew into the airspace above the canyon. It was an exhilarating feeling, watching the ground fall away beneath us as we soared up into the sky, high above the river.

The world looks so different from the air! We all become accustomed to seeing landmarks from the ground, or occasionally, from a mountain peak. But it all looks very different from above. Most people don't get an opportunity to ride in a helicopter. I was thirty-three years old when I first set foot in one that day. I felt immediately disoriented: where were all the familiar landmarks I knew from the ground? *Everything* looked different from a few hundred feet up. The 730-foot-tall Auburn-Foresthill Bridge, normally so imposing, looked small and insignificant below us, like a toy train span. The river canyons seemed to stretch away forever. I could see over the top of the Sierras with the blue of Lake Tahoe glittering on the horizon and the Nevada desert beyond.

"Wow!" I exclaimed.

"Kind of amazing, huh?" the copilot answered. "We really like coming up here. It beats chasing traffic in the valley."

"Do you guys like your job?" I asked.

"Only on days like this!" they laughed. "It gets pretty boring flying up and down the same stretches of highway around Sacramento."

"Where shall we head to?" the captain asked me.

"Out there!" I answered, and we all laughed again. It was during moments like these when I knew I'd made a great career choice.

"We need to map out all possible LZs [landing zones] along the North and Middle Forks of the river," I told them. "Let's start at Oxbow Lake on the Middle Fork and work our way down to the confluence at the Highway 49 Bridge today. Tomorrow, if your schedule allows, I'd like to take a look at the North Fork."

"Works for us," the pilot said. "Only thing is, if we get called away to a manhunt or rescue, we will need to take you back and try again later."

"More reasons for us to fly around again, then," I said.

That first day was incredible. We were out for two hours, flying down into the canyons, sweeping along the river, locking in on the GPS, and mapping points along the river. I could have happily stayed up there for days, but the copilot said they needed to head back for refueling and end-of-shift maintenance.

"Sorry, ma'am, but we'll be back!"

"No worries," I said. "I'm very grateful for the air time!"

In all it took several days of flight time to map out all the LZs along the North and Middle Forks. Sometimes we spotted an illegal mining operation or weed growers I'd never have found any other way. We logged the coordinates, and I worked with ground staff later to go after these criminals. Having a bird's-eye view like this was invaluable.

"How in the hell did you find us way out here?" the hapless miners would ask me, incredulous.

"We have our methods," I'd answer.

"I saw you hanging out of the whirlybird up there the other day!" one of them hollered. "You're not playing fair flying overhead like that! Damn *rangers!*"

I just smiled in reply. He had me there.

We developed a map system with dozens of clearly marked LZs, and this was instrumental in saving lives later.

This has to be the best job in the world, I thought to myself. And to think this was the job no one else wanted. They even had to draft me to do it. Sure, it had its challenging moments, but projects like this made up for the harder moments on the ground.

47.

RIVER TRIP

"I may have to quit my day job to do this from now on," Jordan said jokingly that evening. He loved being on the water and would do it every day if he could. We were camped with our river guide on the Middle Fork of the American River, about fifteen miles upstream from Auburn. The stars were out, sparkling against an inky black sky, with the soft, watery sounds of the river sliding past us. Our tents were up, and our campfire crackled as our guide prepared dinner.

I had invited Jordan along with us on an overnight river trip to help identify camping spots along the river. I had mapped landing sites from the air a few weeks ago, but this information needed to be coupled with on-ground specifics in case we needed to make rescues from rafts.

"You should take Jordan along with you," my supervisor said. "He really knows the river well and has been kayaking it for years."

"Why didn't he take this job?" I asked.

"He didn't want it, none of us did. That's why you're here," he laughed.

"Fair enough," I answered.

I could understand this, after all I'd been through in the past several months. This was no easy job by any stretch of the imagination, but moments like this made it wonderful. Jordan was delighted to be invited along, and he was an invaluable help. He really knew the river well, and had excellent ideas about how to conduct this mapping project. I was content to map a few sites here and there, but Jordan insisted we mark every single spot, in case we needed to know more details later. He was a smart guy and insisted upon perfection with any job done. This could work both ways, because I'd get tired and want to call it a day, and he'd insist we map a few dozen more places.

"Rosanne, there must be at least ten more spots along this next river mile. You don't want to just map one or two of them, do you? What happens if some boater gets hurt between here and the next spot?"

"Okay, we'll capture a few more, but then we need to call it quits for the day; I'm exhausted."

I marveled at his tireless energy. I considered myself a pretty hard-driving person, but Jordan made me feel inadequate somehow. He seemed to have enough training and skills to pass for a Navy SEAL, and he looked just like an Eagle Scout.

We had been working since 7:00 a.m. that morning and it was now 7:00 p.m. I was done for the day. I pulled my rucksack out of the waterproof duffel and yanked out a small overnight bag. This sent both men into peals of laughter.

"What have you got there, designer luggage? Check it out, Steve, she has a burgundy-colored sack with her bedtime toiletries in it! Rosanne, what else do you really need besides a toothbrush?"

"Can it, guys. I'm going downriver to wash up. When I come back, it's time for lights out. We have an early start in the morning."

"Yes, ma'am!" they laughed.

Sheesh, I thought. *Men!* But it was a great time being at the river.

The next day we started early. No bacon and eggs, just boring breakfast cereal and coffee.

"Couldn't you at least have brought some blueberry muffins?" I said to our guide.

"You hired a guide, not a chef," he replied. "My job is to feed you and get you down the river. If you wanted a chef, you should have brought a different dude along."

"I prefer freshly ground coffee," Jordan said, ever the purist. "And I want a gluten-free bran muffin!"

"Hop in the raft," Steve said as he tossed everything into the dry bag. "We're ready to head out now."

Hmmm, I thought. *If I ever do this again, I'm hiring a river chef to fix us French toast and bacon like I saw the commercial rafters enjoying.* Why did we have cold cereal while they all ate like kings? Just because we were state employees didn't mean we had to eat like mongrels. In fact, I was pretty sure dogs ate better breakfast food than us. It was a tough life being a ranger.

48.
"HALT THOSE BUSES!"

That first summer as Whitewater Rafting Program Manager had gone very well. We made a number of trips on the North and Middle Forks of the American River in our patrol raft, and had a noticeable presence on the river. We checked river gear and enforced regulations to make sure each of the rafting companies kept the right items in their boats. We inspected rafts to make sure they were safe. Sometimes we found very dangerous boats with leaking bottoms, or caught groups with too many people on a raft and not enough life jackets, so we terminated their voyages, escorting them off the river at key points. Disappointed paying guests shouted obscenities at us, as they missed out on their day of fun.

"You damn asshole park rangers! We came all the way from LA to go on this trip! We don't have time to rebook with another company!" they screamed at us.

I truly felt bad for them, but it would have been a lot worse if they were injured or lost their lives.

It didn't take long for the rafting companies to wise up. Once everyone knew we were watching them closely, they complied with the rules. The transport rigs were another problem, though. Jess had warned me about this issue when he left the job in my hands.

"You will need to contact CHP and inspect rafting buses and gear vehicles. I did this a couple of times, and it was a real eye-opener. They drive around the countryside in ancient school buses and gear trucks, which look like they're at least forty years old. Make sure you remember to oversee this part of the program."

I conveniently set this issue aside during that first summer. I just didn't have time to think about it—until the two CHP officers showed up in my office one day. Apparently, my overly conscientious predecessor had called them to "remind" them about this crucial part of the job (after I had ignored his voice mail messages). What the heck was he doing worrying about a job he left behind? Dammit anyway. I had enough to do already. I silently vowed to make a trip down to where *he* worked and cause *him* some grief if this continued.

However, the CHP officers were very polite. It was hard not to like them immediately.

"Hello, I'm Curt and this is Terry. We work the commercial vehicle program for CHP. We've been watching the rafting companies for years now, climbing up and down these mountain roads with rigs dating back to 1940. Let's talk about how we can work together to correct this issue. Otherwise, truckloads of people are going to wind up over the side of a mountain and *you* are going to be responsible for failing to take proper action."

Yikes. How could I ignore this issue when it was staring me right in the face? I looked at my phone and willed it to ring and interrupt this unwanted conversation. It sat there silently, mocking me.

"Pleased to meet you both," I said.

Curt was tall and lanky with salt-and-pepper hair and an easy smile. He was obviously the one in charge. Terry was younger, dark-haired, and more quick-tempered, but also very good-natured. He often liked to make jokes. They were both very kind and respectful to me. I think they could sense my insecurity about being around CHP officers. Most of the ones I'd met before seemed indifferent to park rangers, like we were somehow far less important than they were. Most of them had no idea of the magnitude of our responsibilities. I gave them my best smile, while inwardly cringing at the thought of inspecting vehicles. Vehicle mechanics were something I knew absolutely *nothing* about. I felt like a clueless idiot in their presence. They must have read my thoughts.

"We can do all the heavy lifting, so to speak," Curt said. "We'll be the ones doing the inspections. We just need State Parks' approval to do this because this is your program, and we need your presence on the scene. We plan to set up vehicle diversions for inspections."

"Where do you propose to set up these diversions and what will happen? Won't the drivers and their bus occupants object to the process?" I asked with trepidation. I knew how these things could turn ugly. I'd made countless vehicle stops and it was never pleasant, much less stopping big buses and gear rigs for inspections.

"Oh, they'll raise *holy hell* on the spot. They'll come flying out of their rigs screaming and hollering. But we have the authority to inspect any commercial vehicle on the highways, especially after watching these deadly junk fleets rattling up and down the mountainsides."

"Okay, I'm in," I responded. What choice did I have? They were right.

The following week we set up roadblocks on Highway 49 near the Gold Discovery Park in Coloma, and on Highway 193 near Georgetown where they always drove past, transporting people and gear from the rafting company camps on the South Fork of the American River to the launch points on the North and Middle Forks. We also set up a point along Ponderosa Road on the North Fork. Our aim was to set up early in the day and catch them by surprise. This was long before cell phones existed, so they couldn't easily warn each other without having to double back to camp or find a pay phone. Some of them wised up and spotted us before they rolled past, but most of them were caught in the net before they could react.

As we began conducting these inspections, I couldn't *believe* the things we discovered. It was frightening. Terrifying. Unconscionable. These companies were carrying people up and down steep mountain roads in rickety school buses that were retired decades before. Some of the rigs had no brakes. Emergency doors were blocked with rafting gear. Some buses didn't have seats in them, just benches lined up along the walls, and no seat belts to secure riders as the rigs careened around sharp turns.

"Put your foot on the brake when I tell you," Curt would tell the bus driver. Then he would watch in horror as brake oil squirted all over the engine manifold. Terry was underneath the rigs checking their brake lines.

"You have almost no brake pressure! What were you thinking, imperiling people's lives in this thing?" Curt shouted at the driver.

"We didn't know," the driver said.

"Get out of that bus. Everyone off. This rig is terminated!"

"What do you mean, terminated? What the hell are we supposed to do? Our trip is scheduled to begin in less than thirty minutes."

"You should have considered that before you rolled this sorry excuse for a bus out of the shop. Better yet, you should get a new bus!"

"Damn you, f-ing cops!" the guests shouted at us.

I walked over to the group as they cursed the CHP officers, hoping the friendly ranger approach might calm them down. "Folks, I'm very sorry for your inconvenience. But these people were imperiling your lives. They were driving you around in buses with no brakes. Would you rather have rolled off the mountainside?"

"F—-you!" they shouted in response.

Oh well, I thought. No use arguing with them. I did understand their frustration, though. It wasn't their fault they'd booked with an irresponsible company.

We did this all summer, moving to different points along the various routes to the river, trying to outsmart the drivers who took alternate roads to avoid being inspected. But eventually, the rafting company owners realized we were not going away. During large group meetings, I handed out copies of the vehicle requirements and explained what would happen for failure to comply.

"Any company driving people in unsafe vehicles, and any gear vehicles operating in an unsafe manner will be terminated. Additionally, your companies will be *fined* $500 for a first offense, and $1,000 for a second offense. There will be no third offense, because your rafting privileges on the river will be revoked."

This was very unpopular, but we left them no choice, either comply or go out of business on the American River. By the following spring there was a huge transformation in rafting company vehicles. We saw very few problems after that. The district superintendent was so pleased with the way the whole program was going that he put my name in for a California State Parks award for program excellence. His recommendation was later approved, and I was honored along with other award recipients in a formal ceremony that fall.

That year I also worked with the Department of Boating and Waterways to create a map and brochure called *A Boating Trail Guide to the North and Middle Forks of the American River*. We took a series of topographic maps and converted them into a usable quick reference map with helpful information about boating safety that everyone could understand and enjoy. It took months of teamwork to create it, but this guide is still in use today, twenty-five years later.

49.
OFF TO DISCOVER GOLD

I came to love my job as Whitewater Rafting Program Manager. It was a groundbreaking job and an incredible adventure. I worked there for eighteen months. I managed my own time and had my own staff. My commute to work was five minutes, just over a mile from home. I worked four days a week from 8:00 a.m. to 6:00 p.m. I was all set to attend a river rafting guide school and was really looking forward to the experience. There was no good reason to leave, except that I wanted to promote. Even so, I figured it would have to be a pretty darn good job to get me to move. I was happy.

Then one day the opportunity came: the Chief Ranger position at the Marshall Gold Discovery State Historic Park in Coloma, California. The beautiful Coloma Valley on the South Fork of the American River! It was a place I loved and had been going to all my life. Plus, it was only a thirty-minute drive from home.

I interviewed for the job along with at least forty other candidates. I already knew the park superintendent and had worked with him on previous occasions. We completed training assignments together. I felt comfortable with the idea of working with him. The interview went very well. I did extensive preparation, going way beyond what was expected, studying every aspect of the job, visiting the park, talking with the staff, volunteers, and community members there, and going over possible interview questions. I thought very carefully about my presentation. I felt like I really had a chance.

The day after the interview, I was out on the river raft all day long. When I got back to my office at the end of the day, my supervisor told me that the park superintendent at Coloma had called.

"Call him back right away, Rosanne. He's been trying to reach you all day."

My heart was pounding as I called him back. I reached him just as he was leaving his office for the day. His deep baritone voice boomed over the line.

"You almost missed me today. I'm glad you called."

A long pause.

"You want to come be our Chief Ranger at Coloma?"

"*Yes!*" I answered, with all my heart.

"Welcome to the job!"

"Thank you so much; I am so excited!"

"You're welcome. You gave a great interview. I'll contact your boss and work out the details for your start date."

So ended one of the happiest days of my life, and the beginning of a whole new adventure.

I'd come far since my early days as a National Park Ranger at Marin Headlands in California, and at Mount Rainier National Park in Washington State. Experiences working at places like Hearst Castle, Sutter's Fort, and the California State Railroad Museum also helped to shape my career. But the years between 1986 to 1989 at Folsom Lake and the Auburn SRA had really transformed me. I had become a rough-and-tumble patrol ranger. Venturing into the remote canyons of the American River taught me how to embrace adventure. Whether it was bumping down a backroad in a four-wheel drive truck, gliding down a trail on a mountain bike, hiking into the canyon on foot, or cascading down the river on a raft, I was ready to face whatever lay ahead.

This was the other side of being a park ranger: the patrol aspect I had never imagined. Certain parks, like state recreation areas, held a heavier responsibility to duty, requiring a stronger resolve. What you wanted to do, and what you had to do, could be very different things.

When I first chose this career, I didn't envision becoming a law enforcement officer, but in these parks, it was a calling. We had to commit ourselves to being the best. We weren't exempt from the hardships and tragedies we witnessed, but we did have to step up to the challenge. Sometimes it was tough, but most times park visitors were just happy to see us. Whether we were rescuing a lost child, pulling a struggling swimmer from dangerous waters, disarming a dangerous criminal, giving life-saving aid to an injured person, or just being present when someone needed a hand, so many people told us:

"Thank God you're here!"

Thank you to the men and women rangers who risk/risked their lives every day.

This book is a tribute to all the dedicated people I worked with to protect our parks and serve the people who came to visit them. It was a tremendous privilege to stand with other fine park rangers who gave fully of themselves and who were deeply committed to their mission. Each ranger had a different approach to the job, and each ranger was an individualist. This rugged individualism is what drew us to the job in the first place. I was proud to be a ranger, and proud of all the rangers I was fortunate enough to serve with.

My Stetson hat sits on my bookshelf today to remind me, as a cultural icon, of what it means to be a park ranger. To me, it was the greatest job in the world.

ACKNOWLEDGMENTS

Many thanks to my husband, Vernon McHenry, for sharing his stories of being a park ranger with me. A big thank you to my editor, Heidi Eliason, for her excellent assistance. To Joan Chlarson, for creating the artwork for the book cover. Thanks to Eric and Paula Peach for sharing the park maps and park history stories. Gratitude to my son, Tristan McHenry, for reviewing and commenting on the book draft from a park ranger's perspective. Thanks to my daughter, Cameron McHenry, for her insights. Many thanks to my friends, Jan Chapralis, Charly Rallojay, Karen Ho, and Sue McLaughlin for reviewing and commenting on the initial draft of the book. A big thanks to my friends Tricia Slattery and Lynne Shubunka for their multiple readings of the draft book and doing a final proofread for me.

The Gold Country Writers group has provided invaluable help with book-writing critiques. Special thanks to Libby Taylor-Worden, Tzeli Triantafillou, Allison Arredondo, Dora Cividino, and Mary Boyle for their excellent input. Thank you to Joan Griffin for her expertise on book launching and outreach. Thank you also to Jeane Fleck for helping to create the title for this book, to authors Denzil and Jenny Verardo, to Certified California Naturalist Kitty Williamson, and to National Park Ranger Clifford Collier for their reviews of this book. Appreciation to Michael G. Lynch, author, and former superintendent of the Auburn State Recreation Area, for providing photographs of ranger staff, and to author

Jordan Fisher Smith for the photo of us at the Auburn State Recreation Area ranger station. Sincere thanks to Michael G. Lynch, Clifford Collier, David R. Boyd, Barbara Moritsch, and Jordan Fisher Smith for writing such thoughtful and insightful book testimonials. To all my dear friends and family: my gratitude is immense. Thank you for helping me bring this book from concept to reality.

ABOUT THE AUTHOR

Rosanne S. McHenry has served as a U.S. National Park Ranger and a California State Park Ranger over a lifetime career. Her ranger experiences include the Golden Gate National Recreation Area, Mount Rainier National Park, The California State Railroad Museum, Sutter's Fort State Historic Park, Auburn State Recreation Area, Folsom Lake State Recreation Area, Marshall Gold Discovery State Historic Park, and Death Valley National Park, among others. During her career she received several awards for exceptional public service.

Her first book *Trip Tales: From Family Camping to Life as a Ranger* talks about how family camping experiences as a child inspired her to become a U.S. National Park Ranger. This book has received national and international acclaim, earning the Nonfiction Authors Silver Award, achieving Gold Medal Finalist status in the Next Generation Indie Book Awards, and as a four time Finalist in the International Book Awards.

In her latest book, *Tales from a Rogue Ranger*, McHenry shares her experiences about the rough and tumble life of a patrol ranger near Auburn, California. It has been praised by park professionals as an outstanding example of what it takes to work in this field.

McHenry currently lives and works in California, with her husband. The beautiful American River Canyon is adjacent to their home in the Sierra Nevada Foothills.

You can learn more about her at www.triptalesbook.com.

Contact Info:
RangerRose123@gmail.com